The pages ahead exemplify

What Makes Iowa…Iowa

THOSE who haven't visited Iowa often envision it as a vast stretch of flat land…with corn, beans and barns sprinkled across the horizon.

The photos and features in this book offer evidence that nothing could be further from the truth.

While Iowa doesn't have mountains, ocean views, sandy beaches, redwood forests or the Grand Canyon, there are areas of the state with scenery that's breathtaking. This book takes you on a "tour" of those places, with pictures so vivid you'll feel you're *there*.

Without even buckling your seat belt, you'll visit northeast Iowa and wander the steep bluffs and narrow valleys called "Little Switzerland".

Turn the pages and you'll travel across the state to the Loess Hills, where those incredible windblown dunes rise above the Missouri River Valley.

Let your fingers do the traveling and you'll soon find yourself along the quaint, idyllic backroads of southeast Iowa, where you slow for Amish buggies and admire fields of oat shocks.

Then head to the level land of the north-central part of the state where…well, we'll let the following pages do the talking and touring from here.

And what's *best* about Iowa? The answer's easy: The best thing about Iowa is its *people*.

As a whole, they're honest, hardworking, unpretentious, churchgoing, no-hands-out folks who take a great deal of satisfaction in earning their own way in life. They have an uncomplicated perspective: They feel God didn't put them here to be lazy.

They look forward to each season. They know where milk comes from and which way is north.

They're not afraid to get their hands dirty if that's what it takes to get the job done. They enjoy doing the right thing. They define neighborliness.

You'll meet many of these people here and listen to their stories, as though you were leaning over the fence chatting on a no-hurry day.

In short, to really *know* Iowa, you have to *experience* Iowa. So turn the page and begin your tour.

> *"The best thing about Iowa is its people…"*

Linda MacBride

Cathie Houck

Brittany Peiffer

OUR IOWA

Its Beauty...Its Bounty...Its People

Editor Roy Reiman
Art Director Mary Sailer
Our Iowa **Editor** Rick Jost
Copy Editor Kristine Krueger

All Rights Reserved. Published by *Our Iowa* magazine
1510 Buckeye Ave., Ames IA 50010
Phone: 515/232-0075
E-mail address: *editors@OurIowaMagazine.com*
Web site: *www.OurIowaMagazine.com*

ISBN: 978-0-692-05340-9

Front Cover: Madison County farm, photo by Justin Rogers
Back Cover: Delaware County farm, photo by Gerald Rowles

For additional copies of this book, order with a credit card
by calling **515/232-0075** or online at *www.OurIowaMagazine.com*.
Price per book: $16.98 plus $4.98 shipping and handling.
(Shipping is a *flat rate* of $4.98 no matter how many copies you order.)

Stanley Buman: next page and pages 6-7: Gerald Rowles

Pssst...
Something's Hidden In This Book!

SUBSCRIBERS to *Our Iowa* magazine know we like to add a little fun to each issue by hiding something within the pages, then award prizes to the finders.

So, we decided to add that same intrigue to this book. *Somewhere* in these pages we've hidden a tiny "I", a small version of the I in the *Our Iowa* logo.

It looks like the one at right—but remember, that's just a *sample*. The one we hid is much smaller, and it could be hidden in an article, a photo, an illustration or in a headline (nope—we didn't use it as an exclamation point!). But it's there, hiding somewhere in this book.

If you find it, send a note naming the page where you found that elusive needle to: *Our Iowa*, 1510 Buckeye Ave., Ames IA 50010. **Deadline: May 14, 2018.**

If you've identified the correct page, we'll put your entry form along with the others into our cracker barrel for the prize drawing. Only one entry per person.

What's the prize? It's a tasty one! We'll have Amish farm woman Ruby Kuhns send you one of her famous pies, baked fresh and shipped overnight.

Plus, the winner will receive coupons for *free custard from Culver's for a full year!*

So, start searching...and good luck!

This Book Makes a Great Gift
FOR additional copies of this book, call **515/232-0075** and have your credit card ready, or order online at *www.OurIowaMagazine.com*.

Or write to: Coffee-Table Book, *Our Iowa*, 1510 Buckeye Ave., Ames IA 50010.

Price per book is $16.98 plus $4.98 shipping and handling. Shipping is a flat rate of $4.98 no matter how many copies you order.

Like Us to Visit You Regularly?
IF you enjoy what you read in this book, why not subscribe to *Our Iowa* so we can "visit" with you every other month?

Call 888/341-5878. Our friendly operators can help you 8 a.m. to 10 p.m. Monday to Friday and 8:30 a.m. to 5 p.m. Saturday.

Or you can subscribe online at *www.OurIowaMagazine.com*. Click on the "How to Subscribe" link.

Why I Love Iowa Best

By Coe Pettit

I've been to California, that wondrous state of gold;
I've seen the Rocky Mountains, their majesty unfold.
I've seen great New York City, her buildings and her throng;
But 'cross the Mississippi, that's right where I belong.

Some sing of Bonnie Scotland, for there their hearts are tied,
Some sing of sweet Killarney, for Ireland is their pride.
But I will sing of Iowa, that beautiful rich land,
If you could gaze out o'er her, I'm sure you'd understand.

I thought I'd like to travel, I thought I'd like to roam;
So to realize my dreams, I wandered far from home.
Now since I've seen the others, I know what I like best;
I'll take my good old Iowa, and they can have the rest.

Our Scenery's Super In All Four Seasons

WHERE is "God's Country"? For many folks, it's wherever they live. It's human nature to deem your part of the country the very <u>best</u> place to live.

Those in the desert areas of the Southwest laud that they don't have to put up with cold and snow...but they're reluctant to bring up those 100-days-of-100-degrees summers when they can't grab the door handle of their car and have to hurry home when the groceries include ice cream. And every day is pretty much like... yesterday.

Then there's the folks down in the Southeast who tout their mild days throughout the year... but don't talk about the hurricane winds that do a load of damage all too frequently...and the humidity that does wonders for women's hair. Or that they spend 50% more on pesticides than northern states because the frost doesn't penetrate enough to kill all sorts of crawling things down in Dixie.

And the Ivy Leaguers in the New England area? Well, to them that's pretty much where everything really worthwhile is happening. Life is exciting and challenging, and if you can make it there...

For Iowans? Most like things just as they are. They enjoy the change and challenge of the four seasons. They'd be a little bored with the yearlong sameness.

Weather is constantly on their mind and their lips, because it affects their lives directly or indirectly. Yet each season is welcomed with the differences it presents.

They enjoy the quiet of winter...the get-it-planted rush of spring...the sun-filled days of summer...and the bring-it-home days of fall.

Scenery-wise, each of the four seasons brings with it a beauty that is "purely Iowa". You'll find plenty of photo evidence on the following pages, beginning with the prettiest season of all...autumn.

Joseph Stanski; previous page: Don Poggensee

Gerald Rowles

Joseph Stanski

Joseph Stanski

SPRING, SUMMER, FALL AND WINTER. Iowans enjoy the change and challenge of the seasons...each of them for a different reason.

Iowa Autumns Are Awesome!

The kaleidoscope of color from river to river can take your breath away.
Join us for a photo tour along backroads to sights you'd not likely find on your own.

If you ask Iowans to name their favorite season, most will quickly answer, "Autumn". They look forward to fall more than any other time of year, for a lot of good reasons.

It's not just the multihued foliage and crisp air as they ease into November's nip and pull-up-the-covers nights. It's *harvesttime*.

It's when farmers finally collect on the long hours they've put in since last spring, and the rumbling of combines is heard dawn to dusk—and beyond—from Shenandoah to Dubuque.

It's when urbanites in Urbandale climb in the car to see what the season's Artist has done…painting the countryside gold, scarlet and orange with a hint of green. This trek is likely followed by a stop at a mom-and-pop diner for down-home food and a chat with the locals.

It's also when Iowa's best photographers head to the backroads for just the right shot. Until you find time to make such a trip of your own, take the one shared on the colorful pages ahead. See Iowa at its best…in autumn. 🌐

COLOR YOUR WORLD. Pink pumpkins make an appearance at a squash stand in Fayette County.

Gerald Rowles

NOBODY'S HOME. Corral fences add Western flavor to a Midwest autumn in northeast Iowa. Maybe the occupants went to check out the view.

WARM OCTOBER GLOW. A golden sunrise bathes fields in Dubuque County (left). A farmstead (below) is nestled behind the corn.

This photo and previous page: Gerald Rowles

COME AND GET 'EM. Wagons full of pumpkins—and squash by the pound—tempt buyers at a Madison County stand.

SNEAK PEEK. A look over the top of sun-soaked field grass reveals a tidy red barn in central Iowa. From the looks of the weather vane, the wind's out of the east today.

EASY IN THE BREEZE. A crew in a sailboat enjoys a luscious autumn backdrop while cruising near shore at Lake MacBride State Park in Johnson County.

BIG VALLEY. Spectacular fall foliage is captured from an observation deck at heavily wooded Backbone State Park in Delaware County.

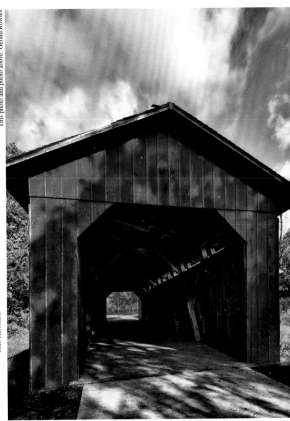

SO LONG, SUNSHINE. Iowa sunrises and sunsets are irresistible to photographers. Here, the fading sunlight creates a mesmerizing purple and peach light show near Mount Vernon.

CRIMSON CROSSING. The far opening spotlights colorful leaves at the wooden covered bridge at Easter Lake Park in Polk County. These timber-truss spans create old-fashioned charm.

Jordan Foster

FIELD DAYS. It's a made-to-order day for harvesting corn near Menlo in Guthrie County. Under bright skies, farmers pick their grain and haul it for delivery to the local elevator.

T. Scott

RED OCTOBER. Get the rakes and bags ready. Ruby-hued maple leaves blanket a wooded lot in Iowa City.

Joan Burns

Gerald Rowles

LITTLE BIT O' HEAVEN. Fiery foliage, powder-blue skies and jade-green grass create an inviting and comfy picnic spot at Lacey-Keosauqua State Park in Van Buren County.

EYE IN THE SKY. A drone hovers above Winterset City Park and captures an eagle's view of 25-foot-high Clark Tower. The tower was built in 1926 as a memorial to Madison County's first pioneer family.

CHEWIN' UP THE SCENERY. What a pretty fall day for a moo-vable feast in the country. These cattle have it made in the shade as they chew up the scenery amid a grove of mature ash trees in rural Butler County.

TURN THE PAGE and you'll see cottonwoods in all their golden fall glory standing sentinel over East Lake in Dickinson County. The benches sure look inviting!

OUR IOWA

IOWA EYE-CATCHERS

*Favorite photos from our readers...
and the stories behind them.*

That's Using Your Head

"WE HAVE a wonderful place to see and photograph birds in our area at Lake MacBride State Park," notes Jerry Peterson of North Liberty. "They maintain a bird blind and raptor center for general public use. This woodpecker was caught on camera, busily pecking a tree near the bird blind."

Future Looks Bright

"A GOOD FRIEND, Katie Mennenga of Ackley, took this photo of her son, Blake," reports Terri Luehring, our Tama County Hawk-Eye. "We have no doubt that he will someday farm with his family, as he just loves to be out in the fields helping with the tractors and combines."

Steep Hill Steeples

"WHILE ON a fall trip around Iowa last October, we happened upon this serene and beautiful Iowa landscape, west of Bellevue," says Janet Abrahamson of Centerville.

Heaven's Gate

"I GREW UP ON A FARM," Taylor Daubenberger explains, "and when I saw this gate, it brought back wonderful memories of my childhood—the beautiful colors that surround the harvest season. This luscious, leafy spot is in Mitchell County, just south of St. Ansgar."

Sunbeams Over the Beans

"I TOOK THIS fall harvest photo and everyone was telling me I should send it to *Our Iowa*," writes Jacob Grodahl. "This is my dad combining soybeans at sunset, near our family farm in Lytton."

Falling In

"MY GRANDDAUGHTER, Juliana, enjoys the great Iowa fall as she plays in the leaves," writes Barb VanDusen of West Liberty. "Of course, playing in a big pile of leaves is a whole lot more fun than raking them up!"

GOT AN EYE-POPPIN' PICTURE? If you have an appealing photo of Iowa's beautiful scenery or that depicts Iowa life, send it to: "Iowa Eye-Catchers", *Our Iowa*, 1510 Buckeye Ave., Ames IA 50010.

Or e-mail it to: *editors@OurIowaMagazine.com* and put "Eye-Catchers" in the subject line.

Make Way for the Pumpkin Train

"FALL IS my favorite time of year for going to the local orchards," says Debbie Heisler of Farley. "And now I just love sharing it with my grandson, Callan. It looks like it may be his favorite time of year, too, as he pretends to drive this lawn tractor."

The Prettiest Farm in Iowa

Nothing symbolizes our state like proudly primped and painted farmsteads. We showcase one of the prettiest in each issue of Our Iowa magazine.

GROWING UP, Louie Zumbach never imagined his family's dairy herd would someday be the inspiration behind this issue's "Prettiest Farm in Iowa".

Coggon•

Louie and his wife, Deb, live on this pretty corn and soybean farm near Coggon, where eye-poppin' red-and-white farm buildings and landscaping beds filled with nostalgia bring a sparkling splash of color to the Linn County countryside.

"I have to credit my dad for the color scheme around here," laughs Louie. "I grew up on a dairy farm nearby where we raised registered Ayrshire cows.

"Dad painted his buildings red and white to match his cow herd. So, when Deb and I bought this farm in 1992 and began adding buildings, we carried on the tradition as a way to remember my parents."

"Howdy, Neighbor!"

Louie and Deb grew up on farms across the road from each other but attended different schools.

"Louie asked me out once when we were in high school, but that date didn't go so well," chuckles Deb. "Things went much

HAPPY TO BE HOME. With four daughters and a son-in-law and plenty of community work to keep them on the go, Louie and Deb Zumbach cherish a rare quiet day at their farm home near Coggon.

better when he asked me out again years later, and we married in 1988."

The couple has four daughters—Allison, Rachel, Taylor and Brandy, who is married to son-in-law Michael—and the family has made good use of the modern horse barn they built in the ↘

OLD CAN BE PRETTY TOO...like the vintage barn and Oliver tractor at left. Below: "Bud" (left) and "Peppy" are much too busy for horseplay today.

REMNANTS FROM THE SHED. A rusty cream can and a wagon that has seen better days provide a reminder of the past in one of Deb's landscaping beds. Below: Morning sunlight streams through lingering storm clouds over the Linn County farm Louie and Deb bought in 1992.

A FAMILY PROJECT. Louie and Deb made many improvements while raising four girls on this farm that the couple bought from a retired farmer.

READY TO RUMBLE. Farm equipment has changed a bit since three Zumbach brothers from Switzerland settled in this area in 1883.

early 2000s. The barn, with handsome cupolas atop the roof, is home to horses "Peppy" and "Bud".

"All the girls were active in 4-H, so the barn came in handy for raising their projects—sheep, cows, bottle-bucket calves, pigs and golden retriever dogs," Louie explains.

"Now that our last daughter is out of high school, Deb's ready to claim part of the barn as her garden shed."

Looks Good as New

One of the brightest buildings on the yard is also the oldest—a traditional red barn with a white roof. Adorning one end is a striking barn quilt that Louie gave Deb as a birthday gift.

"A neighbor lady painted it," says Deb. "Louie looked through her book of designs and picked it out himself."

Nearby is a tidy landscaping bed filled with washed rock, hostas, daylilies and geraniums. Sitting proudly among the flora is a restored 1950s Oliver Super 77 tractor.

"My great-uncle opened an Oliver dealership in Monticello in the 1920s, so my dad and grandfather used Oliver equipment on their farms," Louie relates. "The first tractor Dad bought new—an Oliver Super 88—also sits in the yard near one of the sheds."

Another bed, lined with odd-shaped rocks removed from ⇗

A TASTE FOR RUSTIC. Deb tends to the landscaping, and enjoys giving a rustic look to the beds with her decor. By midsummer, a colorful array of perennial and annual flowers brightens the yard.

AN EYE ON THE OUTDOORS. Louie and Deb watch the changing of the seasons from this cozy sunroom. When they're longing for the company of the girls, they simply enjoy their tender group photo on the wall. Below: The stone retaining wall is a beautiful accent to the yard.

fields over the years, holds a rustic and ornate cupola that graced another old barn that burned in 1993.

Head to the large backyard accented with leafy shade trees and lush beds of hostas, and you're treated to a peaceful respite protected by a pretty windbreak.

An attractive stone retaining wall off the house creates a spacious area to hold perennial and annual flowers, colorful bushes and evergreen shrubs.

The back door of the brick home—built in 1970 by the previous owner and later enlarged by the Zumbachs—opens onto a shaded patio that's ideal for relaxing on summer evenings. But when nights get chilly, the family can enjoy the warmth of a fire in a fire ring nearby.

Stewards of the Land

Louie and Deb recognize the importance of conservation in their operation—waterways and filter strips protect the soil and water across the land that they farm.

Pollinator plots of 11 and 20 acres planted to wildflowers and milkweed provide nourishment for bees, birds and butterflies as well as nesting areas for wildlife.

"I truly believe it was divine intervention that led *Our Iowa* to feature our farm," says Louie. "As I mentioned, we try to keep things up here to honor my parents, and my mother passed away 2 days before we were contacted by the editors asking for permission."

There aren't any Ayrshire cattle in sight today, but Mom and Dad would be mighty proud of how Louie and Deb have turned this place into one of the Prettiest Farms in Iowa. 🏠

FOR HORSES AND 4-H. This barn was built for horses, but the girls found it a handy place to house other 4-H animals too. Below: The retired barn and silo strike quite an impressive pose near the road.

AND THE SEARCH GOES ON...for the "Prettiest Farm in Iowa". If you have an attractive farmstead (or know of one in your area), send us a few snapshots and a letter describing it. If we choose to feature it, we'll send out a professional photographer to take pictures for a future issue.

Mail to: "Prettiest Farm", *Our Iowa*, 1510 Buckeye Ave., Ames IA 50010. Or e-mail: *editors@OurIowaMagazine. com* and put "Prettiest Farm" in the subject line.

Photo next page: Gerald Rowles

DEVIL'S BACKBONE is what they call the craggy ridge that runs through Backbone State Park in Delaware County. Sure is a heavenly sight!

Iowa's a Great Place To Raise Kids

THAT'S especially true for kids who grow up on a farm. For a lot of reasons.

For one, there's a lot of open space out there. Don't have to worry about traffic, strangers and something to do. Actually, there's *work* to do—things they can help with at almost any age.

Farm kids know early on they're part of the "team" that operates that farm. They know people and things depend on them—a calf that needs to be fed, a garden that needs to be watered; they're being counted on.

For parents, there's a big difference between playing with kids and working with them. You're doing things *together*. Kids know they're contributing to the mutual effort and that it has a direct effect on the family's well-being.

Paige Baade

You can even check a kid's attitude when working with him. If you say to your boy, "Help me move this feed bunk over there," you can detect whether his end comes off the ground willingly or begrudgingly.

It's good for kids to learn the satisfaction from honest work...doing things that need to be done and are worth doing. And there are lots of opportunities for that in Iowa.

It's a great place to raise kids.

RuthAnn Zimmerman

Michele Reiman

Joseph Stanski

TIME TO BE CAREFREE. A mom and daughter leave their worries behind—if only for the day—as they saunter down the road that winds through Lacey-Keosauqua State Park.

Gerald Rowles

Stanley Buman

Gerald Rowles

ONE OF IOWA'S SUPREME STREAMS is the 156-mile Upper Iowa River—these canoeists paddling past its forested bluffs in Winneshiek County will sure vouch for that!

BASKET CASE. With so much colorful produce from which to choose…why it's enough to make your head spin deciding exactly what to take home from this farm stand.

This photo and next page: Gerald Rowles

OVER HILL AND DALE, autumn colors of every hue have descended upon the Loess Hills of western Iowa. The only other place in the world you'll find a geologic formation like these wind-blown dunes is in the Yellow River Valley of China.

STONEWALLING we aren't—this rustic fence along the timber's edge is located at Bellevue State Park in Jackson County.

TURN THE PAGE and take a hike along a leaf-strewn trail at Backbone State Park. The photo's so vivid, you can almost hear the crunch of leaves beneath your feet, smell the foliage and feel the gentle breeze on an awesome autumn day in Iowa.

Hawkeye History That May Even Amaze Iowans

Toni Kelleher; next page: Joseph Stanski

Here's a host of fascinating facts about our state that are unknown by most Iowans. See how many are news to you.

EVEN IF you were born in Iowa and have lived here all your life, we're betting there are bits of Hawkeye history here you were unaware of before.

For example, did you know that the Rathbun Dam and Reservoir is the largest body of water in the state…that Wright County has the highest percentage of grade-A topsoil in the entire nation… and that Iowa is the only state in the U.S. whose east and west borders are 100% formed by water?

Here are many more Iowa facts:

● Iowa is the only state name that starts with two vowels.
● Dubuque is the state's oldest city.
● The state's lowest elevation point—at 480 feet—is in Lee County.
● Fort Atkinson was the site of the only fort ever built by the U.S. government to protect one Indian tribe from another.
● Ripley's Believe It or Not has dubbed Burlington's Snake Alley the most crooked street in the world.
● Eagle Grove has an artesian well that has run nonstop for over 100 years.
● The state's smallest city park is situated smack in the middle of the road in Hiteman.
● Sabula is the only town in Iowa that's on an island.
● Spirit Lake is the largest glacier-made lake in the state.
● Iowa's longest and highest bridge crosses Lake Red Rock.
● Kalona has the largest Amish community west of the Mississippi River.
● West Okoboji is the state's deepest natural lake at 136 feet.
● Scranton is home to Iowa's oldest water tower, which is still in service.
● At 16 miles, East Okoboji is the state's longest natural lake.
● Quaker Oats in Cedar Rapids registered the first trademark for a breakfast cereal in 1877.
● Iowa's oldest continually running theater is in Story City.
● Clarion is the only county seat in the exact center of the county.
● Dubuque is home to the only county courthouse with a gold dome.
● Cornell College in Mount Vernon is the only school in the nation to have its entire campus listed on the National Register of Historic Places.

● The Sergeant Floyd Monument in Sioux City honors the only man to die during the Lewis and Clark Expedition.
● Iowa's only fire tower is located in Yellow River State Forest.
● Knoxville's National Sprint Car Hall of Fame and Museum is the only museum in the country dedicated to preserving the history of sprint car racing.
● Wright County has more artesian wells than any county in the state.
● Iowa's only operating antique carousel is located in Story City.
● The St. Francis Xavier Basilica in Dyersville is the only basilica in the U.S. situated outside a major metropolitan area.
● Of Madison County's six covered bridges, Imes Bridge is the oldest and Holliwell Bridge is the longest.
● Elkhorn has the largest Danish settlement in the U.S.
● Crystal Lake is home to a statue of the world's largest bullhead fish.
● Strawberry Point is home of the world's largest strawberry.
● The world's highest double-track railroad bridge is the Kate Shelley Bridge located in Boone.
● The Fenelon Place Elevator in Dubuque is the world's steepest and shortest railway.
● Clarion is the only town that can claim John Phillips as its local hero.
● Iowa State University is the oldest land-grant college in U.S.
● With his six terms—1983 to 1999 and 2011 to 2017—Terry Branstad became the longest tenured governor in American history.
● The Cedar Rapids Museum of Art houses the world's largest collection of Grant Wood artwork.
● Iowa is a Native American word for "beautiful land".

A NOTEWORTHY COMMENT. *"Iowa was such a beautiful country. I loved my villages, my cornfields, the home of my people, and that's why I fought so hard for it. It's yours now. Please keep it as we did."*

—Chief Black Hawk after surrendering in the Black Hawk War

*Favorite photos from our readers...
and the stories behind them.*

Indian Summer Afternoon

"IT WAS such a beautiful day," says Jessica Parsons of Monticello. "So after school, my children and I went to Central Park here in Jones County to enjoy the weather and the fall leaves."

Putting It All on the Line

"THAT'S my dad and mom, John and Carol Miller of Graettinger, with Dad's 16 antique tractors—not counting the one with a loader raised high that I stood in for taking the picture," writes DeeAnn Bates of Estherville. "Dad starts each one every spring, but this is the first time he's had them all lined up."

Pigtails and Pony Rides

"OUR 2-year-old great-granddaughter, Jentry Craighton, was off to help with the horse chores," notes Jill Krause of Slater. "She knows all of the horses by name, but her favorite is her pony 'Dusty'. She loves to go riding...with her mom leading Dusty from another horse."

Happy Scamper

"THIS little fella was eating one of our apples while perched on our birdhouse," explains Rose Schmidgall of Mediapolis. "I snapped the photo in mid-bite, so it looks like he's smiling."

GOT AN EYE-POPPIN' PICTURE? If you have an appealing photo of Iowa's beautiful scenery or that depicts Iowa life, send it to: "Iowa Eye-Catchers", *Our Iowa*, 1510 Buckeye Ave., Ames IA 50010.

Or e-mail it to: *editors@OurIowaMagazine.com* and put "Eye-Catchers" in the subject line.

Deer in the Headlights...err, Sunlight

"THE SUN was setting as I spotted these deer grazing in a freshly combined field," writes Susan Zeman of Manilla. "I was so glad I had my camera so I could share the moment."

Making the Rounds

"ONE MORNING last fall, I woke early on a Saturday, grabbed my coffee and Canon to catch our gorgeous Pottawattamie County in the early light of day," says Kristina Brockhoff of Minden. "Iowa's landscapes are so vividly beautiful—we are blessed to live here."

All Arms and Oars

"OUR GRANDSON Adam Leslie was sitting the wrong way and looked a little awkward his first time rowing a boat," chuckles Ed King of Cedar Rapids. "But with a little coaching from our friend Darrell Morrison, he got the hang of it."

'In Spite of Our Dry Spell, The Crops Look Promising'

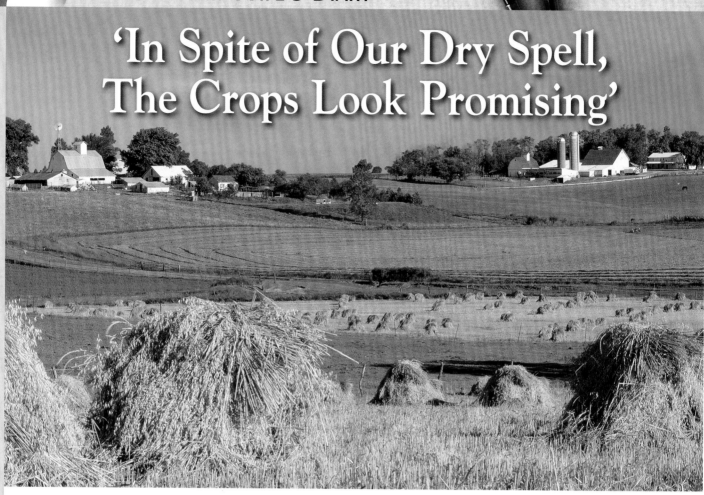

Saturday Diary Entry:
"Although we could use a good rain, we can rest assured that God is in control of the weather."

FRIENDLY summertime greetings from our farm in Wayne County.

I'm Annie Helmuth and I keep a week-long diary in each issue. My husband, Freeman, and I operate an organic dairy farm with our eight children: John, 20, Samuel, 18, Lucy, 16, Esther, 14, Miriam, 11, Lester, 9, and foster daughters Annie Mae, 12, and Clara Mae, 10.

We know summer has arrived when daylight hours turn into long summer evenings…when pastures are dotted with fat lambs…when gangly little colts gallop about on sturdy legs, and momma cows with baby calves nearby are grazing on lush green grass.

On this early summer day, let me take you on a short tour around our farm:

In the farrowing house are 10 litters of less than 1-week-old piglets, sprawled out on bright yellow straw. If you pick one up and it squeals, momma sow comes woofing!

Frisking about in sunshine in the pasture is the 2-month-old filly belonging to our quarter horse "Joy". Curious, the youngster slowly comes to the fence with neck outstretched and ears pricked

"Every bird was praising God with song for another beautiful day…"

forward, a little leery of the two-legged creatures standing on the other side.

Also in the pasture, the dairy cows are either grazing or lying comfortably on verdant turf while peacefully chewing their cuds.

In the barn are young calves nestled in bright straw, their jaws also rhythmically chewing their cuds.

Hidden nearby is a nest from which soft meowing sounds come forth. "Fluffy"

the barn cat jumps up and protectively looks over her family of four. She carries an air of displeasure that we have found her hidey-hole.

Our horses mingle together in another pasture. Some are standing, stomping their feet and swishing their tails to keep the flies away.

Lying in the shade of the porch are "Pepper" and "Sheila", our family dogs, twitching their ears to flick off an ornery fly. Show Pepper a treat, and he's ready to do tricks at your bidding.

Our tour complete, we'll sit in the shade of the big maple tree on the front lawn to rest a spell from our wanderings.

As we sip on fresh, cold garden tea, we'll watch the farm go by while listening to the martins warble and chirp and the buzz of a bumblebee. They're just a small measure of the symphony of sounds that come with life on a farm.

FOR RELIGIOUS REASONS, Amish adults don't wish to have close-up photos taken of themselves. We're honoring that by not photographing our diarist. Instead, we're showing scenes of what you'd see while driving through Iowa's idyllic Amish country.

Any farmer will assure you that hearing these daily sounds is the sweet side of farming. If you listen closely on every God-given day, you feel richly blessed!

Sunday, June 4: Guten morgen! It was a calm, peaceful morning to step outdoors and listen to the mockingbirds' many duets. Now and again from across the road, quail were calling. Both were part of a garbled blend of sweet birdsong.

This is our "in-between Sunday" when we don't have church services… but Freeman and I wanted to go to one of our neighbors who had church.

John helped Freeman hitch "Vicky", John's new horse, to the buggy. Vicky thinks standing still to be hitched to a buggy is a waste of time. But once we were on the road, she trotted along briskly.

Church was held in a shop building, and midway through worship services a train rumbled past on nearby tracks.

On the way home, we stopped at another neighbors' place to see their new baby. When we arrived, the younger children were roller-skating out under the barn lean-to; there were still traces of purple on their hands from eating mulberries.

When we arrived home, a partly assembled puzzle was spread on the table and the aroma of popcorn pervaded the air. The whole house had the homey air of a typical Sunday afternoon.

We had time to take a nap before Lester and Miriam rode "Ginger" and "Sugar" to the back pasture to bring the cows up for evening milking.

Lucy and I did the milking. Although it was warm and the cows kept swishing their tails, we cooled off afterward when we washed the equipment.

After supper, the children went outdoors to play; Freeman helped them with pitch and catch.

It's one of those lazy summer evenings

LET'S PLAY! Amish schoolyards will soon be filled with shouts of merriment at recess.

Don Poggensee

when a porch glider is an ideal place from which to watch and hear the day draw to a close. Moonbeams filtered through the maple tree from a nearly full moon. From somewhere deep in the trees came the throaty beat of a tree frog.

Monday, June 5: A delightful, cool breezy morning! It was a refreshing change from the last few days of warm humid weather.

As daylight arrived, it sounded as if every bird was praising God with song for another beautiful day.

When I fixed the boys' lunches, I found an empty cookie jar, so I quickly stirred up a batch of cookies. It kept me scrambling to have their breakfast and lunches ready by the time their driver showed up to take them to their jobs.

Out in the barn, Freeman did the feed-

> *"The cornfield looked like a sea of green as it shimmered in the wind and sunlight…"*

---

ing and scraping while Lucy and Esther did the morning milking.

Lester rode Ginger back to the pasture to bring up the horses so we could use "Duchess" to mow lawn. I heard their thundering hooves as they came galloping up the lane and into the barn.

After breakfast, Esther and Lester moved the portable fence to give the dairy cows a fresh area to graze, and Lucy hitched Duchess to the mower and began mowing.

Meanwhile, I helped Annie Mae and Miriam get started with laundry—it fluttered and flapped in the morning sunshine. Then I made sure the patio flowers all had a drink of water. There's nothing like flowers to brighten up a home.

For some time, Clara Mae has been begging to have a turn at making bread; today was a good day to let her try. She measured and stirred and kneaded dough for six loaves…and was very happy when the bread turned out nice and fluffy!

Today was the day the dairy inspector came for the annual inspection of our organic operation, so I helped Freeman get the paperwork together. There's a lot of required paperwork with being organic, and it seems there are always one or two papers that elude you.

Lester came in after dinner and excitedly announced that sow No. 10 had 13

piglets! They moved some piglets to other sows with smaller litters so they will have a better chance of survival.

From the house, I watched Lester grab his straw hat and take a swing at a bumblebee out under the barn lean-to. He and his trusty hat have outnumbered a few carpenter bees already.

Tuesday, June 6: A cool morning… almost chilly. But a brilliant sunrise soon dispelled any chilliness.

It didn't bother the hummingbirds at the feeder. In fact, the "boss" hummingbird kept quite busy chasing his fellow hummers away when they got too close.

Freeman brought the cultivator up to the barn and put on the rolling shields for cultivating corn. He was hoping the job could wait until the corn is taller, but the weeds are growing, too.

After our morning duties were aside, Lester and Clara brought out seed flats for planting pumpkins. In a few weeks, we'll transplant them in the field. Until then, we'll get them started in flats on a table out on the lawn.

Everyone pitched in to help—Clara Mae and Lester filled the flats with organic potting soil, and the rest of us planted the seeds. We were almost done when we ran out of potting soil. The rest would have to wait until we get more soil at the greenhouse.

I cut out and began sewing a bonnet. Miriam and Annie Mae became interested watching me, then got out the box of patterns to make a bonnet for their doll.

While I was gone to town after dinner, Lester found a big tire in the machine shed. With much effort, he dragged and rolled it up to the walnut tree in hopes of making a tire swing.

At chore time, Annie Mae discovered a spider wrapping up a fly with its silken thread. She quickly came to tell me, but when I arrived on the scene, poor "Miss Fly" was already completely encased.

It was almost dark when Freeman came up from the field. We had a late supper and called it a day.

Wednesday, June 7: Another delightful cool morning. We were all up early because Freeman and I and the two older boys were invited to a wedding.

Freeman got the morning milking started, then he and Lester rode over to the pasture with Sugar and Ginger to put the young dairy heifers back into their proper pasture. Leave it to grazing heifers to find any weak spot in a fence!

John got three horses ready to go to ⤳

Annie's Vegetable Haystack

Bell peppers (diced)
Broccoli (chopped)
Cauliflower (chopped)
Onions (finely diced)
Tomatoes (diced)
Mashed potatoes (warmed)

Lettuce (shredded)
Hamburger (cooked, drained and seasoned)
Salsa
Cheese sauce
Nacho chips (crushed)

Prepare enough diced and chopped vegetables according to how many servings you wish to have. Put in separate containers and refrigerate until serving. (Note: You may add or subtract vegetables of your choice.)

To assemble each serving, take a dinner plate and spread a portion of mashed potatoes in the center. Add lettuce and a spoonful (or more) of hamburger, followed by a small portion of each vegetable. When your "haystack" has reached its desired level, spoon salsa on top and drizzle with cheese sauce. Sprinkle with crushed chips and enjoy!

the wedding. John left an hour earlier than we did because he had to help park buggies when the wedding guests arrived.

Before the rest of us left, I was busy with nameless little tasks that always need to be done—especially on busy mornings when the clock seems to race you.

A few minutes after 7, with the sun shining brightly, we were on the road with "Justin" trotting briskly along. Samuel followed not far behind with his horse "Dawn".

After the sacred wedding vows were spoken and the last song sung, everyone went to the reception at the home of the bride, where all the guests were served a delicious dinner.

Since I've helped as a wedding cook a time or two, I know the effort the cooks put into making the wedding dinner special.

After visiting awhile with friends and neighbors, we followed the dusty road home again.

At home, the girls pulled what was left of the early radishes that had gone to seed, tilled the soil and laid out stakes for staking up tomato plants.

Clara Mae, due to her recent success baking bread, kneaded another batch and again it turned out nice and fluffy!

Miriam and Annie Mae helped Lester put up his tire swing using rope that Freeman used for plowing. The rope kept stretching due to the heavy tire, and after repeatedly tying the knot, they took the tire off and fastened a board to sit on instead.

As soon as we got home from the wedding festivities, Freeman harnessed four horses to cultivate several hours before dark.

Shouts and laughter drifted through the open window as the children played the games of a summertime evening.

Thursday, June 8: It seems we should store these cool early mornings for later this summer when the heat index is high.

With chores and breakfast over, Freeman got the cultivator rolling again. He wants to finish the field by noon.

In the house, we hurried with dishes and morning work because my two sisters were coming to spend the day.

We also planted the rest of the pumpkins in the potting soil John picked up at the greenhouse on his way home from the wedding last evening.

When my sisters arrived, they both brought a dish along—corn bread salad and ingredients for sub sandwiches. Lucy prepared fresh strawberries and a chocolate cake for dessert.

Lester and his two cousins came in for dinner with hands and mouths tinged with purple! It wasn't hard to see they had been busy in the mulberry tree. After dinner, they went back to the pond to catch frogs. Lucy, Esther and cousin Ida Mae hitched

---

> *"Laughter drifted through the open window as children played the games of summertime..."*

Ginger to the wagon and bumped their way to the pond to pick out a good spot for camping someday soon.

The younger girls had a tea party out under the maple tree; thus, the day sped by. By the time my sisters left, Freeman had four teams hitched to four mowers, ready to clip rye in a field already planted to soybeans.

I gave Lucy and Esther the option of milking cows or mowing rye, and was secretly glad when Lucy chose milking.

With Freeman using "Duke" and "Thomas", Esther driving "Rick" and "Rock", and Lester using "Buddy" and "Ug", I took off with "Tim" and "Tina"

and together we all rattled down the lane with our teams and headed for the bean field.

Not a cloud was in sight as we clipped rye 'round and 'round the field. Birds swooped and glided just above the ground, no doubt finding an easy supper.

When we finished, the entire 25 acres lay golden and brown. Hidden beneath the fallen rye, we hoped, was a passel of soybeans bursting at the seams ready to grow.

When I got in, Samuel was lying on the couch; even with the warm weather, he asked for a blanket. I dosed him with some remedies and hoped he'd sleep off whatever was ailing him.

Friday, June 9: It was chilly enough that I closed several windows. A big friendly moon in the southwest slowly disappeared below the horizon.

After the boys were off to work, and with chores and breakfast finished, Freeman shod Sugar's two front hooves.

Then he, Esther and Lester rode Ginger, Sugar and Missy to a neighboring pasture where the grass is growing short due to the drier weather. They sorted 10 of the bigger heifers and herded them along the road to our timber pasture.

As the saying goes among the old-timers of this area: "No matter how much it rains, we are always 2 weeks away from a drought!"

When they got back, Freeman got the four teams ready to mow another 22-acre field of rye that's been planted to soybeans. Lester hurried with some small jobs Freeman had given him so he could take Annie Mae's place mowing rye.

While Freeman, Lucy, Esther and Lester mowed, the younger girls helped me do laundry.

I checked the pumpkins and found

little sprouts, a sure sign they should be popping through any day.

After dinner, I got some things ready to take along to a benefit supper the community is holding to raise money to pay hospital bills for a person in need.

Freeman and I helped with the benefit. It was 13 miles away, so we hired a driver to take us. Along the way, we picked up the ice-cream wagon that runs off a gas engine and freezes 10 gallons at a time.

When we arrived, we saw plenty of smoke as chicken and burgers were being grilled. It was an interesting evening, socializing with others of the community we don't see very often.

Samuel felt well enough that he helped with chores and came with the others after they were done.

Saturday, June 10: Freeman took advantage of the cool morning to finish planting a 14-acre field of beans with a no-till drill. He headed for the field right after breakfast.

A fella with a horse trailer picked up John and a team of our draft horses, Tim and Tina, along with a mower to take to Freeman's brother's place. John plans to help his uncle and several others clip fields of rye today.

Samuel and Lester cared for some little pigs and bedded the hoop building with fresh straw.

Esther and Annie Mae moved three cows ready to dry up to the dry-cow pasture. But the cows were determined to

---

"I made two blackberry pies and got Sunday clothes ready for tomorrow..."

---

stay with the milking herd and were soon back home!

I ran some errands with neighbor Bernice and when I got back, the house was quiet with nobody in sight. They were all outside helping herd 10 sows to the gestation building. I watched the sows amble slowly along. It never pays to hurry a sow!

Lucy and Esther washed several loads of laundry, but the wind almost whipped it off the line.

The wind blew the buggy out from under the barn lean-to, and caught a flat of pumpkins out on the lawn and flipped it over. Some of the seeds fell out, revealing 1-inch sprouts. I replanted them and gave all the flats a good soaking.

I believe I was just as happy as Freeman when he came in from the field, having finished bean planting for this year.

I took slices of bread with fresh freezer jam as a snack to the men in the barn, then watched Freeman dress a horseshoe for Duchess.

The girls shined up the boys' buggy after chores, while I made two blackberry pies for supper and got Sunday clothes ready for tomorrow.

The cornfield across the road looked like a rich sea of green as it shimmered and waved in the wind and evening sunlight.

In spite of our recent dry spell, the crops look promising. Although we could use a good rain, we can rest assured that God is in control of the weather. We'll get our rain and sunshine as He sees fit.

With that assurance, may His blessings shower you with health and happiness! 🏠

Don Poggensee; next page: Robert Buman

GOOD DAY, SUNSHINE. It's a serene evening scene as the sun dips beyond Emmet County's High Lake.

RUBBERNECKING IN NATURE. Alert! In the coolness of a shady meadow near Fort Dodge in Webster County, a white-tailed deer perks up after spotting a two-legged observer.

COMBININ' BEANS. It's the harvest hustle in this field near Spirit Lake, where farmers team up to bring in the bounty of the year's soybean crop.

WALKIN' THE PLANKS. It's a bridge of Madison County, but this one is uncovered, unlike the red-sided spans made famous by literature and Hollywood.

RIVER RUN. Who says leaf peepers need a car? Here, a boat speeds up the Mississippi River near Marquette/McGregor. The photo was shot from a Pikes Peak State Park overlook.

HIDDEN GEMS. Some photogenic nuggets are nestled far off the beaten paths. In this case, orange, yellow and green leaves provide a colorful tree skirt in the woods of Boone County.

WALK AMONG THE MAPLES. You can almost hear the crunch of leaves as a couple takes a quiet stroll on a sidewalk along aptly named Maple Street in Fairfield, Jefferson County.

WAGON HO! In Fayette County, green and red ag equipment (below) work in harmony to harvest.

THE HILLS ARE ALIVE. The Madison County countryside begins to display its autumn finery, as a kaleidoscope of leafy colors is illuminated beneath a striking bluebird sky.

OLD YELLER. A towering maple tree reaches for the clouds and creates a vast yellow and orange leafy canopy in Van Buren County. Such vivid colors on a crisp fall day are like catnip to photographers!

SEA OF BEANS. It's a golden harvest in Greene County, as these soybeans seem just about ripe for the combining. Last year was quite the bean season. Think we'll see another soybean bin-buster this year?

GREAT WAY TO START A DAY. Folks on this Johnson County farm were greeted with a dazzling surprise when they awoke and headed to the barn to do the chores.

Ready?...
Here Comes Winter!

No getting around it—Iowans are a hardy bunch. Many actually look forward to the winter season. The pace is slower and allows a little more time to relax.

Okay, some of you will admit it—you look forward to Iowa winters. Maybe not quite as much as we anticipate the coming of spring, summer or fall, but after the hustle and bustle of those other seasons, winter's a time for many of us to take a deep breath and ease up a bit.

It's a time to slow down and admire the lacy handiwork of Jack Frost on a rosy-cheeked morning…make snow angels with the grandchildren…or go for an afternoon walk in the woods as big flakes of gently falling snow muffle the noisiness of the world. It's so quiet there.

Winter's also a time to head over to the neighbors for a long overdue visit, and maybe bring a plate of cookies with you. Then return home, knowing there's a cup of hot chocolate and chunks of Iowa oak crackling in the fireplace to warm you. There's something so soothing about the heat from a wood fire that can't be beat.

To be sure, sometimes Ol' Man Winter takes a deep breath along with us…and when he exhales, he leaves behind a couple feet of drifted snow. But that's just an opportunity to show how hardy we are. And hearty, too, as we go, shovel in hand, to dig out the neighborhood shut-ins and elderly.

That's the Iowa way.

Daniel Ruf

DIDN'T GET THE MEMO…that winter was coming at Hottes Lake in Dickinson County, where these Canada geese might be "honked off"!

FLOATIN' FLAPJACKS. An unusual phenomenon known as pancake ice forms below the Marble Rock Dam on the Shell Rock River in Floyd County.

ONLY IN IOWA! You might say a creative farmer in Buena Vista County took Christmas decorating to a whole new level by stringing lights on the ladder of his grain bin. Now that's the way to take steps to offer season's greetings to passersby!

KEEPING AN EYE PEELED paid off for photographer Don Poggensee. "I spotted this northern saw-whet owl at Moorhead Park in Ida County," he explains. "Though rare and about the size of a robin, they've showed up here regularly over the years."

SEA OF SNOW BLOWS TO AND FRO. There's not much to hold it back on a cold winter's afternoon on this windswept prairie in Mitchell County.

Gerald Rowles

HITTIN' THE HAY would be mighty inviting in this barn converted into a cabin in Linn County. It has all of the comforts of home...including a couple of stained glass windows, gazebo and plenty of firewood on the porch for a cold winter's night.

Don Poggensee

Gerald Rowles

WINDCHILL? BRING IT ON! Youngsters welcome a stiff breeze as they fly their kites on Clear Lake during the town's annual Color the Wind Kite Festival. The fun happens the third Saturday of February. Pack up your long johns and join 'em!

NATURE'S NIGHT-LIGHT shines brightly over Jasper County. December's full moon is called the Cold Moon—when nights are longest and winter cold fastens its grip.

FEELING THE HEAT—from cutting all that firewood and now burning it. A Dubuque County family has plenty to keep warm.

DOWN THE HATCH. Life's a bowl of cherries—or in this case winter berries—as a cedar waxwing happily pops another one.

NOT SO ROCKY START to winter in Dolliver Memorial State Park in Webster County, where newly fallen snow softens the jagged edges of boulders strewn about Prairie Creek.

TAILGATING takes on new meaning at Big Creek in Polk County, where an angler tries his luck at ice fishing. All he needs is a barbecue grill to prepare the catch of the day.

ICE-SKATING, ANYONE? The smooth-as-glass ice on this farm pond in Tama County looks so inviting for a skating party. And the wonderland in which it's set makes for an exhilarating day.

HIGHLIGHT OF THE DAY, after long hours of working in the cold on a Century Farm in Floyd County, is to head into the cozy warmth, where there's likely a pot of soup simmering on the stove.

TURN THE PAGE and you'll see a winter sunrise over Boone County. Judging by the vane on the old windmill, the wind is blowing out of the south. Hooray—it means warmer weather's on the way!

Paul Sorensen

A CABIN "UP NORTH". What could be a cozier sight than this log home nestled in the woods after a magnificent hoarfrost? This setting in Winnebago County, just east of Forest City, is reminiscent of the rugged pioneer log-home days past in northern Iowa.

This photo and previous page: Joseph Stanski

Joseph Stanski

HEAD 'EM UP, MOVE 'EM OUT! With a north wind blowing snow almost horizontally, George Benson and his cowboy crew push almost 150 head of cattle down from a pasture to the ranch in Deep River during a fierce, nearly blinding Iowa winter storm.

PRETTY PERCH. When you bird-watch in the wintertime, you find the most interesting little houses hiding behind and hanging in trees. Fluffy snow and blue color made this one stand out by an oak in Jefferson County.

CAN'T BUFFALO HIM. A proud American bison—proclaimed the U.S. national mammal in 2016—shoulders the snowfall in Carroll County's Swan Lake State Park.

IN THE PINK. Just enough light left in the day! A vibrant cloud forms at sunset over the snow-coated timber, cropland and hay bales on a Hamilton County farm.

WATERFOWL FORMATION. Common mergansers line up on the ice at partially frozen Blackhawk Lake in Sac County.

WELL-LIT FOR SANTA. St. Nick shouldn't have any problem finding this home in Plymouth County. The owners went to some mighty great lengths to warm up their home in illuminated bright, cheery and festive holiday colors.

HEAVENLY PEACE. The ice begins to form on Don Williams Lake in Boone County, where freshly fallen snow, calm water and misty skies create a memorable winter scene.

TURN THE PAGE for a spectacular view of the Hogback Bridge in Madison County weathering a snowstorm.

LET IT SNOW! On the backroads of Washington County, just outside of Kalona, an Amish horse and buggy trot through the white stuff.

grocery stores with pies and other baked goods.

Since my last diary, we've had to adjust to another change in our lives. Rosalyn has been teaching school, and this year Kathryn has begun teaching, too.

Kathryn's school is about 9 miles from home, so she boards during the week at the home of a family living near the school. She sometimes comes home for one evening.

Our farm has been extra busy because in between their farm work and chores, Jacob and the boys have been building a

"Ernest is quite a daddy's boy..."

new combination freezer-cooler for us. Our old one isn't large enough for the food for our family and all our bakery goods. Plus, our neighbors have been storing frozen food in it as well.

The new one measures 16 by 32 feet. There's still some work to do on it, including going to Dubuque to get a used freezer door that then needs to be installed.

Earlier in the year, we had too much rain for our tomatoes and they weren't doing very well. But since the rains have slowed down, they've greened up and are just loaded with big and small tomatoes. For the first time this summer, we have all we want to eat.

If nothing happens to them, we should have plenty to finish the rest of our canning. We still want to can around 100 quarts of ketchup, 50 quarts of pizza sauce and 30 quarts of tomato soup. Plus, we want to can some soups for Grandpa.

Whenever I go out to the garden and see all those tomatoes hanging on the plants, I feel so rich and blessed. It reminds me of a saying I've been repeating a lot lately: "How to get rich quick—count your blessings!" How true.

Sunday, Oct. 4: We woke to a cloudy, cool morning.

Ernest slept longer than usual this morning, so I finally got him up at 8 a.m. to get him dressed for church. Here in our community, the little boys wear dresses until they are a year old—a dress is cooler

'We Had a Rodeo When the Neighbor's Cows Got Out!'

Wednesday diary entry: "One cow came in our driveway and ran after Paul Harvey. Jacob cut her off, and she charged him, pinning his leg against the silage chopper. That was close!"

CHEERY GREETINGS from our corner of the world here in the Amish community of southern Davis County.

I am Ruby Kuhns and I keep a week-long diary in each issue of *Our Iowa*. My husband, Jacob, and I have been blessed with 12 children: Kathryn, 22, Rosalyn, 21, Edna Marie, 19, Paul Harvey, 18,

Regina, 17, Galen, 15, Wilbur, 13, Loren, 11, Matthew, 8, Luke Allen, 6, Jeremy, 5, and Ernest, 1.

We live on a 170-acre dairy farm and raise hogs, too. We have an in-home bakery and bake for the farmers markets in Muscatine and Davenport from May through October. We also supply several and makes it easier to change diapers.

But he celebrated his first birthday a few weeks ago. So now for church I dress him in his white shirt, dark gray pants and a small vest.

He started walking about 2 weeks before his birthday and is almost running now. He has such a mischievous look as he teases and tries to run away from us.

With it being so cool this morning, we all wore socks and shoes—all except for Ernest. I haven't gotten his shoes down from the attic yet. And he probably wouldn't like them anyway. At his age, our other children thought they couldn't walk wearing shoes if they'd started walking barefoot.

So I just put socks on him, and once at church, I took them off—they were too slippery for him to walk.

Ernest was fidgety during church services as he got tired of sitting on our laps. He wanted to go to Jacob and wasn't happy until I took him over to the men's side of the room, where Jacob and the boys were sitting. He's quite the daddy's boy!

On the way home, Ernest sat on Jacob's lap in the buggy and helped drive "Rita". He loves holding the reins in his hands while driving down the road. And Rita doesn't seem to mind a bit!

Shortly after we'd arrived home, Loren came running in and said our white heifer had a new little heifer calf. That makes six heifer calves for us and just one bull calf so far this fall. One cow even had twin heifer calves, which is doubly exciting.

Several of the girls' friends and cousins came home from church with them this afternoon. Tonight they went back for supper and singing.

Jacob and the boys chored earlier than usual so we could get over to Harvey and Betty's house, along with two other families, for supper and to see their new little baby girl.

Monday, Oct. 5: After breakfast and our usual family devotions, Kathryn and Rosalyn packed their lunches and got their things together, then left for their schools with a local taxi driver. With Kathryn staying all week, she had a lot to get ready.

Edna Marie gathered up all the dirty laundry and washed it. Regina washed dishes and packed school lunches for the schoolboys. After that, she made a gallon of yogurt.

Jacob and the boys had a very busy forenoon. Grandpa wanted to start har-

vesting corn and beans sometime this week, so the gravity wagons needed to be unloaded; they were full of corn Jacob and the boys shelled from last year's ear corn still in the crib.

The livestock needed more hay, and there was forming to be done to pour concrete for a pad for our new freezer. The foam insulation crew came and sprayed the walls of the freezer. They didn't have enough foam so said they'd come back and finish tomorrow.

One of the neighbor boys came with a field tiller to do some tilling for us, and Jacob had to help him get started. So our farm was just teeming with activity today!

I caught up on the mending pile, then sewed a pair of pants for Ernest that I'd cut out last week. He has only two pair of everyday ones—Jeremy had worn out most of the hand-me-downs. I want to sew four more for him.

Ernest wasn't very happy, so Regina took him along up to the attic to get his shoes to take him outside since it was too cold to go barefoot. He threw a big fit

---

"Rosalyn, Regina and Paul Harvey went to an apple snitzing..."

---

when we put on his shoes and socks, and I finally took him outside to get his mind off his feet.

We checked the tomatoes to see if they should be picked again, then I showed Ernest the chickens and the new calves. I helped him pet them and he loved it.

But when we returned to the house, he still didn't like his shoes. So I took them off, and he fell asleep while I fed and rocked him. While he napped, I was able to work on his pants and had them done by lunchtime.

After lunch, Jacob and the boys finished forming the pad, then shelled more corn out of the crib until the load of concrete arrived. They all helped with that, and it was suppertime when they finished.

Jacob was floating the concrete to get it smooth, but it was starting to get hard. So he had Luke Allen and Jeremy take turns sitting on the float for more weight, while he pulled it back and forth across the surface.

The schoolboys brought home their report cards, so I took time out from sewing to look at them, which I always look

forward to doing. Later, Jacob looked at them and signed them.

After supper, I cut out two more pairs of pants for Ernest. I thought about cutting out some pants for Paul Harvey, too, but it was 8 p.m. and I decided to sit down and relax a little before bedtime.

I sat in my favorite chair and read some in one of my favorite magazines called *The Little Red Hen News*. It is mostly about making soaps, tinctures and salves.

Paul Harvey, Rosalyn and Regina went with the youth group to John Earl and Susan's for an apple snitzing tonight. Sister Susan said they had 14 bushels to cut up; tomorrow she'll can them for applesauce.

Tuesday, Oct. 6: Regina had made tomato gravy, sausage and corn bread for breakfast. Plus we had homemade grapenuts for cereal with strawberries and cake.

Jacob has a scratchy throat and wanted some hot tea. I made a pot of our own tea, which we grow in the garden and cut off and dry to use in the winter.

Once chores were done, Paul Harvey spent all day sowing timothy hay with the seeder in the field where we'd chopped corn for silage and that had been tilled yesterday. The timothy is for a cover crop this winter and hopefully a harvest next spring. He didn't quite finish before dark.

The girls and I cut up 2 bushels of apples for applesauce. We had some of our own Cortland and Ozark Golds, plus some Yellow Delicious from the neighbors. We got a little over 30 quarts and should now have enough with the 80-some quarts we canned earlier this summer from our Lodi apple tree.

This afternoon Edna Marie went to Grandpa's house and did his laundry, then she picked three 5-gallon pails of tomatoes and tilled the west garden. I helped her sow oats in it by hand for a cover crop.

Jacob was kept busy this afternoon with other people. First the foam insulation crew came and finished insulating the new freezer. Next he had to load our kitchen refrigerator on a truck for delivery to the service man, who will give it a whole new refrigeration unit. We'd had it repaired twice before this and it still wasn't working.

Before he was done loading it, another man drove in to talk about building another hoop building for the hogs, which we hope to do before winter sets in.

Jacob and Galen ground and unloaded two more batches of feed for the hogs. They then finished shelling the last of the

Ruby's Pumpkin Dessert

1 cup pumpkin
1 cup cream or evaporated milk
3 eggs, beaten
1 cup sugar

4 teaspoons pumpkin pie spice
1 box yellow cake mix*
3/4 cup butter, melted
1 cup chopped nuts

Combine the first five ingredients; pour into a 13-in. x 9-in. baking pan. Sprinkle dry cake mix over the top; drizzle with melted butter. Sprinkle with nuts. Bake at 350° for 1 hour or until done. Serve with ice cream or whipped topping.

*I often substitute a recipe for yellow cake. I mix all of the ingredients, then add 1/2 cup of softened butter and mix until crumbly. This works really well.

FOR YOUR HOLIDAY GATHERING, try Ruby's pumpkin dessert. Just the aroma of pumpkin baking in the oven creates a festive air.

corn. The crib is finally empty.

We were happy to have Kathryn come home tonight. It was quite lively in the house with the girls and me talking.

Kathryn and Rosalyn both had some school papers to check, so when the boys were done choring, Wilbur, Loren and Matthew helped them.

Ernest is in his glory during evenings when everyone is around and he gets lots of attention, especially from the boys who play with him.

I was hungry for popcorn, so Wilbur popped a popper full for Jacob and me before he went to bed.

Wednesday, Oct. 7: Kathryn left for her school at 6:30 and Rosalyn at 7:30.

This is laundry day again, so Edna Marie washed and hung it outside. After that, she tilled and sowed oats in the north garden. I'm so glad that is done now.

Regina washed dishes and cut up three-quarters of a bushel of tomatoes, added parsley, onion and peppers to cook for a batch of pizza sauce to can. She also helped me with Ernest; he was grouchy and wanted someone to hold and play with him all the time.

I had several hours of bookwork to do, then worked on another big mending pile from yesterday's laundry.

We had quite a rodeo here this morning when some of our neighbor's wild beef cows got out. Neighbor Mose had just bought them and had them delivered to his farm yesterday. When he let them out of the corral this morning, six of them, each with a little calf, went through the electric fence and were on the road and in a field across the road.

Galen rode "Carmen" up to help the neighbor's two boys, who were also on ponies. But they couldn't do a thing with them as they'd charge the horses.

One cow came running in our driveway, in and out of the horse barn and then ran after Paul Harvey. Jacob cut her off, and she charged him, pinning his leg against the silage chopper as he scrambled up the chopper to get away.

That was close! I was glad I didn't see it happen.

Back to the horse barn she went, where Jacob, Paul Harvey and Galen penned her in. Mose and his boys came down with a team and wagon, and between all of them, they finally got a halter on her so Mose

---

" Paul Harvey took some horses up to Grandpa's and helped harvest his corn..."

---

could pull her home behind the wagon. But not without a struggle all the way as she dug in her hooves while the horses pulled.

Our dog "Fritz" is a good livestock dog, but he couldn't do anything either. Every time he nipped at the cows' heels, they whirled around and came after him. Mose finally ended up calling some cowboys with horses and dogs to round up the rest of them this afternoon.

Edna Marie, Regina and I were so busy with our mending, housework and garden this afternoon, and were happy to see the schoolboys come home—now we had a babysitter. Ernest is always so excited to see them, and Matthew took him outside to play.

Luke Allen gathered the eggs, then I

showed him how to carefully wash them and put them in cartons. He felt important to be entrusted with that job.

Jacob's leg felt pretty sore, so he rubbed some liniment on it before going to bed.

Thursday, Oct. 8: Today is a "bake day" for the Saturday farmers markets. By breakfast time at 5:40, I had all of the ingredients ready to mix for my first batch of cookies. Meanwhile, Edna Marie and Regina mixed all of the quick breads except for the strawberry rhubarb bread.

Jacob thought they could spare Wilbur from the chores to help me mix cookies since Kathryn is teaching. With seven batches of cookies to mix and Ernest to take care of, I appreciated his help and we had five batches mixed by the time Ernest woke up.

After breakfast, our helpers, Sara Louise and Rachel, came and with all of us pitching in, we baked the cookies, breads, muffins and 12 angel food cakes.

This afternoon we made pie fillings and measured out the ingredients for the dough for tomorrow's baking. I also baked eight loaves of peach cobbler bread, which is something new for us this year that has been selling very well.

So has another new item—pumpkin angel food cake.

Jacob's leg was really sore this morning, but it takes a lot to hold him down and he went out to help chore. After chores, he helped the boys get the corn picker and horses ready to start harvesting at Grandpa's today.

Friday, Oct. 9: I fell back asleep after the alarm went off—then woke up with a start and sailed out of bed thinking it was late. To my relief, it was only 3:45, but still high time to begin baking pies for tomorrow. ⇨

I quickly woke Regina, but Edna Marie was up already. A little later, I woke the three oldest boys; I wanted them to help carry in all the big stockpots and bowls of fillings and dough from the freezer.

Jacob usually helps with that, but with his lame leg, I was concerned he couldn't carry. He said it felt better this morning, though.

Despite our slightly late start, we had a batch of 60 pies completed and a second

---

"After the work was done, the older children talked and laughed until bedtime..."

---

batch of 54 almost done by the time Paul Harvey made breakfast.

By lunchtime, we and our four helpers also made 115 small pies, over 100 loaves of bread, 75 pans of rolls and 12 pans of pumpkin bars.

After lunch break, it was time to finish up—bag and label everything, put icing on the rolls and pumpkin bars and, of course, wash all of the dishes. After supper, we loaded the trailer for the trip to the farmers markets early in the morning.

Paul Harvey took some of our horses up to Grandpa's today and helped him harvest corn. Galen put on a rain suit and cleaned the pig nursery with the power washer to get ready for another group of little pigs coming in next week. Jacob did some more work on the new freezer.

Kathryn and Rosalyn came home and we had fun catching up. And after all of the work was done for the evening, the older children sat in the kitchen and laughed and talked awhile before going to bed.

I feel so relaxed tonight with everything ready to go tomorrow morning!

Saturday, Oct. 10: At 2:30, I woke the girls—Edna Marie, Regina, Kathryn and our helper Luann—who are working at the farmers markets today. The van arrived at 3, Jacob helped hook up the trailer and by 3:20 they were on their way.

It was a beautiful clear morning, but cold at 42°. Rosalyn made biscuits and gravy for breakfast. Warm biscuits are delicious with butter and honey!

Paul Harvey helped Grandpa harvest corn all day; they finished up by 5 this afternoon. Galen and Wilbur worked around our place with Jacob.

I'd made a list of cleaning jobs in the house for the other boys. Luke Allen and Jeremy finished their lists first and helped Loren and Matthew. Rosalyn cleaned the bathrooms and the two girls' bedrooms upstairs while I washed the dishes and cleaned the two ovens in the kitchen.

The afternoon sped by with laundry, tidying the sewing room and baths for the boys. Before I knew it, it was suppertime and the girls arrived home from the farmers markets. They reported a good day, for which we were thankful.

Oh, what a good feeling to have another week of baking behind us. Just three more to go and we'll be done with the farmers markets for the year. The girls were disappointed when they discovered we have one more weekend than they'd thought—October has five Saturdays!

So closes another week of life on the busy Kuhns farm. God continues to watch over us and gives us many blessings. What a mighty God we serve! 🏠

SWOOPING IN. Ty Smedes caught this great shot of a snowy owl gliding over a snowy field in central Iowa.

Gerald Rowles

Joseph Stanski

Gerald Rowles

DECK THE BARN WITH BOUGHS OF HOLLY—or in this case a festive Christmas wreath. Why, it's enough to make the cows come home!

GIVES YOU GOOSE BUMPS to think about taking a dip in the partially open waters at Lake of Three Fires State Park in Taylor County, but this gaggle of Canada geese doesn't seem to mind a bit.

MAKING TRACKS in Boone County. Critters making these tracks aren't living on the wrong side of the tracks—not with these cedars for shelter.

70

OUR IOWA

PRETTY PASTELS color the morning skies and a lone tree laden with hoarfrost as the moon softly sets over flat farm fields of Marshall County.

HEADIN' TO GREENER PASTURES—well, maybe not yet. But at least these cattle are being herded to protection of the barn after an early-season snow in Poweshiek County.

WHAT A SPOT TO SKATE. Rusty-red seasonal cabins are reflected in the ice of Lake Icaria in Adams County. Skaters could have quite the time on this big smooth patch!

OUR İOWA

MELLOW YELLOW warms the landscape as the sunrise streams across Big Creek Lake in Polk County, offering the promise of another great winter's day in the state we love.

Gerald Rowles

Ruth Pickle

Gerald Rowles

Gerald Rowles

HALLOWED GROUND sleeps under a blanket of white at Ingemann Church in the Loess Hills of Monona County. The Danish pioneer church is a treasure trove of history.

MOOORY CHRISTMAS! Only on a country road in Iowa will you see a holiday lights display like this one! We were kinda tempted to call it a "manger scene"…but we won't.

72

This photo and next page: Gerald Rowles

WATER OVER THE DAM sure looks cold, but "Old Man River just keeps rolling along", even on this winter's day at Lock and Dam No. 12 at Guttenberg. The lock and dam system makes commercial river navigation possible—just one tow of 15 barges carries about 1,050 semitruck loads of cargo.

BERRY GOOD MEAL. Cedar waxwings can be found in Iowa year-round—including in winter when they feed on berries.

TURN THE PAGE to witness a dramatic sunrise that reminded our photographer of a scene from the Serengeti in Africa. But no—it was taken right here in Iowa at Saylorville Lake.

Phooey on Those Pretty White Flakes!

Snow loses its luster for diarist whose winter slowly "goes south".

WE published this diary in our Feb/Mar 2010 issue, but so many new subscribers have joined us since then that we thought they'd enjoy it...and some of our early ones would enjoy it again.

A COUPLE from Iowa kept a diary early this winter and sent segments of it regularly to close friends in Florida. Here's how the diary went:

Dec. 1: Bill and Sarah, thought you'd like to know why we're "staying home" here in Iowa this winter.

As you're well aware, we spent the last five winters near you there in citrus land. But we so missed the seasonal change, the pure white snow and the scent of the pine trees that we decided this year we're going to stay in our cozy home and "enjoy winter".

Dec. 5: We certainly made the right decision! The first flakes fluttered down today. We'd forgotten how beautiful they are.

Dec. 8: More gentle flurries today. Forecast says we may get as much as an inch. We hope so—it will be so pretty to have everything covered with a soft, pure white blanket.

Dec. 10: We got our wish! It snowed 2 inches. It's *beautiful!* Honestly, it looks just like one of those scenes you see on a Christmas card.

It was the light, powdery type. I was able to just sweep the flakes off the front walk and even the driveway. We are <u>so</u> <u>glad</u> we decided to stay here!

Dec. 13: Just as Thursday's snow had mostly melted away, we got another 3 inches. How fortunate we are! It's all white and breathtaking! You don't know what you're missing.

Dec. 15: Oh boy, what a surprise—another 4 inches. I went to Ace Hardware and got a good-sized snow shovel (do you know what they *charge* for those things now?), and after about an hour, I got the walk and drive cleared.

Have to admit I'm aching a little, but it's a good "physical ache".

Dec. 16: An even bigger surprise—two big snowfalls back to back! And speaking of "back", mine's getting a real workout.

I even asked Helen to help me. Together, we eventually got it cleared, and it's now piled pretty high on both sides of the drive. Getting surprisingly cold, too.

Dec. 18: This is kinda unbelievable—the snow just doesn't seem to want to stop. Have to admit, it doesn't seem as pretty now. Due to the low temps—only 6 above—it's all ice underneath. Helen slipped and fell, her back is now sorer than mine, so I have to go it alone.

Even worse, just after I finished, the snowplow driver came by and pushed the end of our driveway shut. But...he's doing his job, so I just shoveled it out again, then went in for three thumbs of brandy.

Dec. 19: Snow's finally slowing, but the temperature dropped even lower. I'd forgotten how cold it gets here this time of year—goes right to the bone. We both went out to buy heavy winter clothing today. Caps with earflaps, mittens, fur-lined boots, the works.

Do you know how much they charge for that stuff now? We hadn't bought any of those things for years.

And then to top off the day, while we were gone, that snowplow jerk went by again and closed the driveway, so I had to shovel our way in!

Dec. 21: This is really something; 5 more inches. We were going to shop for a Christmas tree today, but the way it's coming down, I dunno.

Besides, that darned snowplow came by again, so I would have had another

Illustration: Joe Sibilski

3 feet of the frozen-hard stuff to shovel through.

Dec. 22: I had two reasons to dig out today—the tree, and a trip back to Ace to check out a snowblower. Do you know what they *charge* for those things these days? Man, you used to be able to buy a truck for that kind of price. So forget it, I'll just be a man and get it done with my shovel.

Speaking of *trucks*, that son of a gun went by with that big orange plow again, and I had to dig my way back in the drive! Five thumbs of brandy this time.

Dec. 23: Oh my heavens—it's snowing some more! How's the weather down there in citrus land? I hope it's *raining*.

Helen healed enough to help me, and we both slugged away at it for about 2 hours. She has her own shovel now, and we both have enough calluses to prove we know how to use them.

You're not going to believe this—I think that snowplow guy hides down the street and waits for us to finish! We'd no more gotten into the house and shed all those layers of clothes and here he comes again!

If I'd been able to get my boots on fast enough, I would have run out there and hit his truck with my shovel! Added more brandy to our shopping list.

Dec. 24: Well, no worry here about a white Christmas! Got another 6 inches, it's 4 below zero, wind is at 48 mph. The snow is falling sideways!

The only one who might be enjoying this is that snowplow idiot who whooshed by again 10 minutes ago. I rushed out the door in my stocking feet, crunched through 2 feet of snow on the front lawn and threw the shovel at his truck!

I've had it! Phooey on the snow! Phooey on the ice! Phooey on the cold! Phooey on Christmas! And phooey on you in your warm, green little Florida abode! Don't write—I don't want to hear how it is there. See you next year...up close. 🏠

Daniel Ruf

FROSTED TREE BRANCHES paint the sky on a quiet winter's day in Dickinson County.

Finally, It's Here…
It's Springtime in Iowa

Ahhh, April…we've been waiting for you. Especially gardeners and farmers itchin' to get seed in the soil. So turn the pages—experience spring in Iowa.

Listen…was that *thunder*? We welcome its sound and the scent of a shower with open arms and open windows.

While most Iowans appreciate the variety of weather that comes with having four seasons, including the nip and the challenge of winter, by now they've closed the seed catalogs and are ready to get something growing.

Spring puts a spring in farmers' steps as they hurry to beat the first rain (and likely their neighbor as well). Their year starts here, with a casino-like gamble on the weather ahead.

Gardeners begin work on their soil and their calluses, already envisioning this season's whopper tomatoes. The birds are back (*"Was that a meadowlark?"*), the lilacs are blooming, the kids are tossing the ball about. With sun on their shoulders on a perfect spring day, how could life be better?

Some of Iowa's top professional photographers have captured this magical time of year. So join us via the pages ahead as we take you on a spring tour of our beautiful state.

Gerald Rowles

Stanley Burman

CAREFREE DAYS of spring are marked by larks singing in the meadows and leisurely strolls in parks like Lacey-Keosauqua in Van Buren County (far left).

SPRING'S BURSTING FORTH…even through the bark of this redbud tree…and in the rolling hills of Audubon County (below), where freshly tilled fields await planting to produce the bounty of a new growing season.

Gerald Rowles; previous page: Joseph Stanski

HARBINGERS OF SPRING in the Loess Hills are dainty pasque flowers, also called Easter flowers.

FEEDING TIME for a baby prothonotary warbler. They nest in tree cavities, leading Iowa-born naturalist Aldo Leopold to call the yellow birds "the jewel of my disease-ridden woodlot".

UNABRIDGED BEAUTY is the iconic stone bridge at Ledges State Park near Boone. Built by the CCC, the bridge has ushered in many a spring.

Gerald Rowles

LOOKS LIKE A HIGH MOUNTAIN LAKE—but it's not. Brushy Creek in Webster County is testimony to scenic variety you'll find across the state of Iowa. And there's no better time to explore it than on a sunny spring day with puffs of clouds floating across our mile-high skies.

Gerald Rowles

YOU CAN ALMOST SMELL THE EARTH in this photo of a prosperous-looking farm in Cedar County. There's just something about the scent of rich soil as it reawakens in the springtime.

BETTER LOCK UP THE HENHOUSE! This mama mink would like nothing better than to teach her young about raiding the chicken coop for an easy meal. Mostly, though, they hunt along streams.

Ty Smedes

Gerald Rowles

ON-THE-MARK MONIKER. These flowers are called spring beauties—and they sure are! You'll find them blooming in many of Iowa's woodlands.

OUR İOWA

Joseph Stanski

LIKE AN OASIS. After a tough winter, this pool surrounded by forest in Lacey-Keosauqua State Park in Van Buren County is a welcome sight!

Stanley Buman

This photo and next page: Gerald Rowles

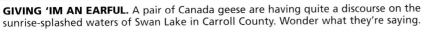

GIVING 'IM AN EARFUL. A pair of Canada geese are having quite a discourse on the sunrise-splashed waters of Swan Lake in Carroll County. Wonder what they're saying.

DON'T CLOUD YOUR THINKING—use your imagination to visualize what kind of object you see in these clouds. To us, it looks like a lambkin bouncing over the green horizon.

TURN THE PAGE for a pastoral spring scene in Story County. Fortunately sheep like dandelions as well as grass—note how few of them are left on their side of the fence!

*Favorite photos from our readers...
and the stories behind them.*

Reaping What She'd Sowed

"I'D SPENT many hours planting tulip bulbs in the fall," writes Polk County Hawk-Eye Lindsay Meleshko. "Thankfully it paid off, as we had many blossoms like this beauty blooming along our fence in the spring."

Scrambling for Eggs

"OUR GRANDSON Justin likes to gather the eggs from my hobby flock of chickens," explains Janet Abrahamson of Centerville. "On this particular day, he didn't need the basket to bring in his take. Just two eggs—c'mon, girls!"

All Is Well in Carroll County

"WE sorely needed rain and watched a shower pass a couple miles to the south of us," relates Mary Phillips of Manning. "It rumbled and rumbled, but all we had to show for it was this spectacular rainbow. But then that evening, we received nearly 2 inches. It was awesome!"

No Nibbles—No Matter

"I SNAPPED this photo while fishing at Lake Considine near Dumont," notes Cody Freese of Sumner. "The opportunity to spend such a beautiful spring day outdoors made up for the lack of fish caught!"

Catering to the Cats

"OUR GRANDDAUGHTER Addison spends most of her time in the barn feeding the cats when she comes to visit," says Deborah Hastert of Harlan. "On this occasion, the cats had had their fill and were ready for a catnap. No amount of coaxing from Addison could entice them down."

Ah—the Scent of Plowed Ground!

"TIME WAS when moldboard plowing was a rite of spring," notes Greene County Hawk-Eye Peg Gannon. "Tom Hammel of Jefferson was among a group of antique tractor enthusiasts who got together to bring back the sights, sounds and scents of that era—if only for a day."

A Ducky Day After All

"I WAS out taking pictures of birds and was getting discouraged because I didn't see many," says Kathy Peck of Storm Lake. "I snapped this blue-winged teal almost as an afterthought, but when I downloaded it, I was pleasantly surprised at how pretty it is. I especially like the reflection."

Julie Habel

NO ARTIFICIAL DRYER SCENT NEEDED—not when you can line-dry the laundry when the ol' backyard apple tree is in full bloom.

KISSED BY THE SUN. With the bright sunshine beaming through them, the petals of these tulips appear on fire, adding warmth to any yard.

LOVE'S IN THE AIR. Covered bridges, like the Cutler-Donahoe in Madison County, are called kissing bridges. Many a smooch is stolen inside.

FIELDS OF DREAMS—and we're not talking the famous baseball field. Newly planted land in Marshall County offers hope for a bountiful crop.

ROUGH AND TUMBLE GAMES. It's all in fun for these coyote pups outside their den in the Des Moines River Valley. The playfulness is in stark contrast to their mournful cry at night.

LIGHT AT THE END OF THE TUNNEL is springtime. Good thing, because you wouldn't want to travel this low-maintenance Level B road in the Loess Hills of Harrison County in winter.

OUR IOWA

Stanley Buman

STILL WET BEHIND THE EARS. With its big doe eyes, a newborn fawn gives a curious glance at our photographer in a Carroll County woodland. Cute little fella, isn't he.

TIME FOR RECESS...and playing "ring around the rosy"—tree, that is—at North River Stone Schoolhouse in Madison County. The walls of this historic school aren't likely to "all fall down". They were built of native limestone in 1874 and are still standing.

Gerald Rowles

Clint Farlinger

Ruth Pickle

A LUCKY DAY when swallows nest above your door. Beside being cute, they're said to bring good luck.

OUR Iowa

Gerald Rowles; next page: Daniel Ruf

CIRCLE OF LIFE. Amid decaying logs in an old-growth forest in Clayton County, northern maidenhair ferns brighten the forest floor and signal renewal on a misty early-spring morn.

RINGING IN SPRING are these Virginia bluebells. You'll find them growing wild in the moist, rich soils of Iowa's woodlands.

TURN THE PAGE and you'll witness a dramatic sunset over the fertile farmland of Dickinson County. Former Iowans, particularly those who live in the shadows of the mountains or live amid the canyon walls of big cities, say they miss Iowa's mile-high skies. With scenes like this, it's easy to see why!

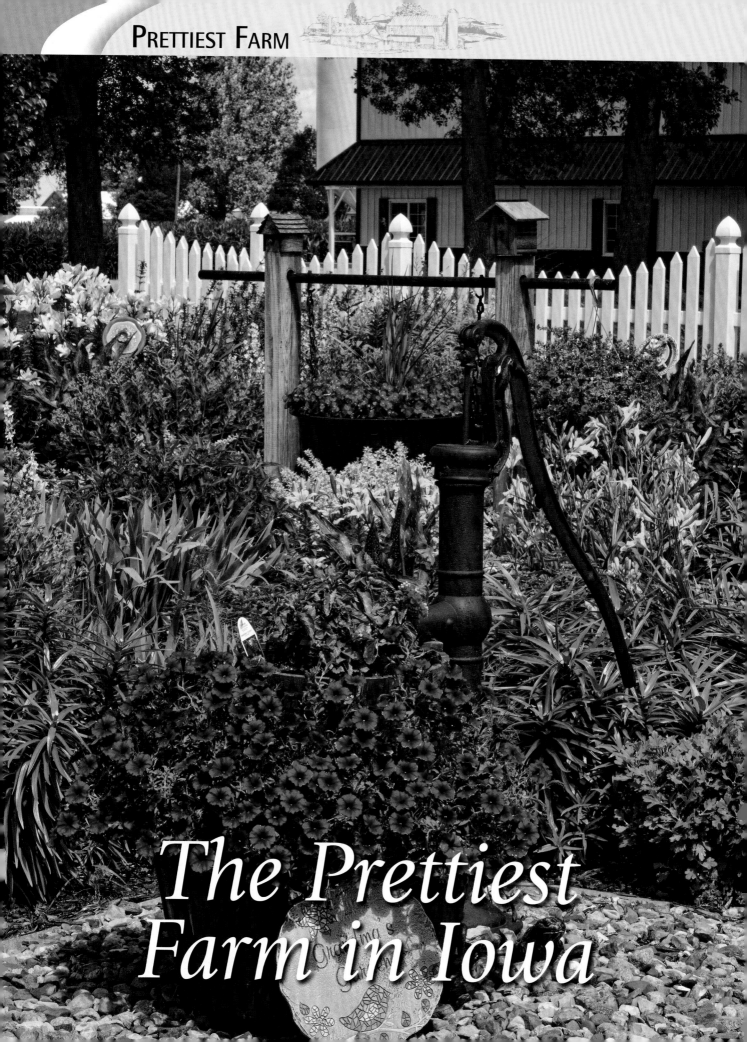

The Prettiest Farm in Iowa

Nothing symbolizes our state like proudly primped and painted farmsteads. We showcase one of the prettiest in each issue of Our Iowa magazine.

AS HIGHWAY and business expansion near Waterloo crept closer to John Weber's old family farm in the 1980s, his dad suggested it might be time to move the center of their farming partnership farther away from the city.

Dad's foresight was spot on. John and his wife, Kathy, had already moved south to a new farm in Tama County after they married in the early 1970s, then in 1987 purchased their current farm and home just west of Dysart. While Waterloo continues to grow, they find life wonderfully serene today on this issue's "Prettiest Farm in Iowa".

"We still farm land around Waterloo—about 20 miles north of here—and land south of here near Clutier," says John. "Buying this farm near Dysart turned out to be a real blessing, because it's centrally located to our entire operation."

John's primary focus after graduating from Iowa State with a degree in animal science was to farm and raise hogs with his dad. Kathy grew up on a farm 9 miles from John near Hudson, but the couple only knew each other casually through Black Hawk County 4-H meetings.

"We began dating after meeting at a church get-together at Iowa State," says Kathy, who majored in art education.

"My dad had a purebred seed stock hog operation and I would have liked to have gotten an ag degree like John, but that wasn't so common for women back then."

Loved Grandma's Gardens

Kathy ended up with the best of both worlds. Besides doing

THEY LIVE HERE FOR A SONG. Birds of all feathers find a safe and welcome home on the John and Kathy Weber farm west of Dysart.

some teaching, she's enjoyed working alongside John and raising their four children on the farm, while using her artful eye to paint a pretty picture around the meticulously kept farmstead with flowers, trees and landscaping beds.

"My grandmother was of Czech heritage and lived on a farm near Tama, and I always longed for the beautiful cottage gardens like she kept at her home," Kathy explains.

John pitches in to help, too. He enjoys designing landscap- ➔

SHADE YOUR EYES! The old pump at left stands amid a colorful attraction. Below: John and Kathy's '67 Chevelle sure brightens up their yard!

STRETCHING THEIR STEMS. These lilies seem to be reaching for every ray of sunlight they can muster to show off their brilliant blooms. Below: The landscaping is meticulously well-kept on John and Kathy's farm. The handsome American foursquare home was built in 1940.

GRANDMA WOULD BE PROUD. Kathy always admired the cottage gardens her Czech grandmother kept and longed to grow them herself.

ing beds, and has paved several paths winding through them.

The Webers also appreciate the beauty that trees bring to a farmstead—they have dozens of evergreen and deciduous trees growing throughout the yard.

Proud to Be Pork Producers

John and Kathy keep busy at Valley Lane Farms, with help from their son and business partner Brian and several employees.

They finish hogs on contract, and grow seed corn and seed beans for DuPont Pioneer. Brian also operates a Pioneer seed business from the farm.

John has served on state and national pork industry boards. He was president of the Iowa Pork Producers Association in 2010, and president of the National Pork Council in 2016.

Kathy also volunteers for the Iowa Pork Producers and remained active with county 4-H long after the kids left home.

"All our kids were involved in 4-H and worked in our hog operation," says Kathy. "You can't beat that kind of experience for learning responsibility and acquiring leadership skills."

They Cherish Their Heritage

John and Kathy's well-kept 1940 American foursquare home is a handsome reminder of rural architecture of the past. A   ⇒

REFLECTIONS. A gazing ball among the flowers in the large garden captures the sun and its "burst" plus these pretty pink ladies.

BIRDHOUSES AND HOSTAS. You'll find plenty of both in the shade of dozens of young and mature trees kept neatly trimmed around the yard. Right: John's shop doubles as a museum of family treasures. His dad bought this John Deere 520 in 1958.

LIVING THEIR DREAM. John and Kathy feel blessed to be able to farm after college. They grew up on Black Hawk County farms 9 miles apart.

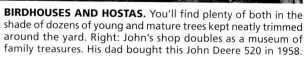

gleaming white wraparound porch was added in 2005.

The home's interior has been beautifully remodeled over the years; the importance the Webers place on faith and family is evident from the home's decor.

A short walk from the house is a modern shop that has become a museum of sorts holding family treasures.

"Our parents left us many heirlooms and artifacts that we cherish," says John. "So, I set aside an area of the shop where they can be displayed for us to enjoy. Our family heritage is alive and well here."

Included in the shop is a John Deere 520 two-cylinder tractor that John's dad bought new in 1958, and a rare JD 4000 that John bought in 1971 when he began farming.

Both tractors—along with a near duplicate of John's first car, a 1967 butternut-yellow Chevelle—are restored to their original factory luster. All that bright color has even the flowers turning their heads with envy on one of the Prettiest Farms in Iowa.

AND THE SEARCH GOES ON...for the "Prettiest Farm in Iowa". If you have an attractive farmstead (or know of one in your area), send us a few snapshots and a letter describing it. If we choose to feature it, we'll send out a professional photographer to take pictures for a future issue.

Mail to: "Prettiest Farm", *Our Iowa*, 1510 Buckeye Ave., Ames IA 50010. Or e-mail: *editors@OurIowaMagazine. com* and put "Prettiest Farm" in the subject line.

FOUR GREEN THUMBS. The Webers share a passion for growing flowers and work together creating beautiful landscaping on the Tama County farm they've lived on since 1987. Below: The wraparound porch, added in 2005, is a shady respite most any time of the day.

Favorite photos from our readers...
and the stories behind them.

Putting Its Right Foot Forward

"THIS MULE FOAL was only 17 hours old and it was already following its mama's lead," notes Curt Swarm of Mount Pleasant. "Even their tails were in sync."

Not-So-Fancy Footwork

"MY AUNT AND UNCLE were taking us on a hayride on their farm near Alden," says Nicole Hemken of Pleasant Prairie, Wisconsin. "My aunt was opening the pasture gate when she lost her shoe in the mud—twice."

Dutch Treat

"SPRINGTIME is tulip time...with brightly colored blossoms dotting many gardens around Iowa," writes Michael Kleinwolterink of Yale. "It's particularly special for those of us who are Dutch."

Rolling Out the Red Carpet

"I AM a real-estate appraiser and travel throughout southern Iowa for my job," says Julie Owen of West Des Moines. "My appraisal of Red Haw State Park in Lucas County when the redbuds are in bloom? Priceless!"

The Iowa Islands?

SURE looks like a collection of islands along a mist-shrouded seacoast. But Paul Sorensen of Forest City explains: "This view of a foggy early-March morning is from the tower at Pilot Mound State Park—roughly 250 feet above the surrounding farmlands. You can see a long way from there."

Puppy Love

"MY SON Sheldon, 4, was so happy when his aunt gave him a puppy," writes Kristal Martin of Osage. "Sheldon and 'Buddy' spend lots of time together playing in the hay shed...and chasing the cats!"

GOT AN EYE-POPPIN' PICTURE? If you have an appealing photo of Iowa's beautiful scenery or that depicts Iowa life, send it to: "Iowa Eye-Catchers", *Our Iowa*, 1510 Buckeye Ave., Ames IA 50010.

Or E-mail it to: *editors@OurIowaMagazine.com* and put "Eye-Catchers" in the subject line.

Got Their Number

"THESE CALVES on our Scott County farm were content as could be just soaking in the sun on a warm spring day," writes Dana Drummond of Donahue.

101

Iowa Weather Forecast:
Artly Cloudy

Mother Nature paints the sky with "art" ranging from puppy dogs to jackrabbits.

SEVERAL issues back, we urged readers to "keep their heads in the clouds"…and be on the lookout for interesting cloud formations that looked like animals, giants or other objects.

We offered a prize for the best photo: a huge, colorful box kite or a check to cover $50 worth of ice cream "floats" at a local stand.

Judging by all of the entries we received, we must have had a lot of readers with stiff necks as they craned to study the clouds and snap photos of them! Here's a sampling—we received so many that we didn't have room for them all.

Carm Fett of Mount Pleasant will likely be on cloud nine when she learns that her photo of a teddy bear waving (left) was the contest winner. Actually, that teddy bear looks like it may be giving Carm a high five to congratulate her!

TEDDY BEAR. "I was living on a farm near Donnellson when I spotted this cloud that looked like a teddy bear," says Carm Fett of Mount Pleasant. "It seemed like it was waving to me."

> **KEEP AN EYE ON THE SKY—** and send us a photo of an interesting cloud formation you see and tell us what you think it looks like. We'll print more of them in an upcoming issue.
>
> Send to: "Cloud Art", *Our Iowa*, 1510 Buckeye Ave., Ames IA 50010. Or e-mail it to: *editors@OurIowa Magazine.com* and put "Cloud Art" in the subject line.

JACKRABBIT. "This sunset made me think of the jackrabbits we used to see years ago on the farm," explains Beth Carlson of Ankeny.

HEART. "My daughter Jennifer Sanders pictured this heart in the west as she was leaving work," notes Linda McClure of Cedar Rapids.

PUPPY DOG. "I saw this billowing dog cloud in the heavens," exclaims Karen Hempstead of Manchester. "All dogs do go to Heaven!"

ANGEL. "My husband passed away and this reminded me of him—my angel husband looking after me," writes Lois Strawn of Jefferson.

OUR IOWA

BUFFALO RIDER. "I first saw the horns, then the cowboy hat and arm flung back as the buffalo bucked," says Patricia Bartie of Sumner.

ARROW. "I hadn't driven in weeks, and this cloud seemed to be pointing to our acreage and guiding me home," says Deb Hastert of Harlan.

STORM FACE. "A storm followed me home. It wasn't until later that I saw the face in it," notes Shelley Larson of Harmony, Minnesota.

WICKED WITCH. "It sure looked like a witch to us—with her face profile and hair blowing in the wind," writes Eugene Melby of Castana.

HEAVENLY HAND. "Mom sees her hand reaching out to Dad's in Heaven," says Sue Hosch of Marion. "It even has her arthritic knuckle!"

DRAGON. "Can't you just see a fire-breathing dragon or monster creeping along the horizon?" asks Sarah Kreutner of Vinton. "Grrrrr!"

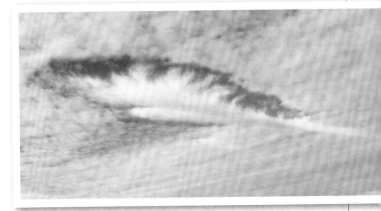

FEATHER. "This is one of the most unusual cloud formations I've ever seen," comments Melissa Adams of Kellerton. "I'm tickled to share it."

FISHIN' WITH GRANDPA—a great way to spend a day, even if the fish aren't biting. They're trying their luck at Ida County's Crawford Creek Recreation Area.

BELLY-DEEP IN GRASS in a pasture in Guthrie County—it's a sight that'll make a cattleman smile. You can bet these cows are pretty happy 'bout it, too!

TAKING THE LONG VIEW OF THINGS. You can see a long way from atop this ridge in Clayton County. Gosh—it's green as far as the eye can see!

Gerald Rowles

HIKE AMONG THE HARDWOODS. The trails are beckoning at Ledges State Park in Boone County. So let's all play hooky today and go for a walk.

PETAL PUSHERS. Hepatica blossoms push up through last autumn's fallen leaves—they're one of the first heralds of spring in forests across Iowa. Beware—the dainty flowers can cause spring fever!

GOING WITH THE FLOW is a bluebird greeting the dawn of a brand-new day in Fayette County.

Gerald Rowles

Gerald Rowles

Gerald Rowles

FANCY PANTS. These wildflowers are called Dutchman's-breeches. (Aptly named, don't you think?) Ants love the tiny seeds and spread 'em by carrying them back to their nest.

Gerald Rowles

Joseph Stanski

Ty Smedes

LONG MAY SHE WAVE. A cemetery at North English in Iowa County is all decked out for Memorial Day. Old Glory never looked more glorious than on a spring day in Iowa!

CHIP OFF THE OL' BLOCK is this baby woodchuck tagging along close to momma. Mom will soon be teaching him the finer points of digging in Grandma's flower beds!

Gerald Rowles

BEATS A SPA ANY DAY. The pooled waters of this stream in Lacey-Keosauqua State Park in Van Buren County are sure to soothe the spirit after a long Iowa winter. Wouldn't it be fun to just sit and dangle your feet in there?

THE LAND BETWEEN TWO RIVERS. Iowa is 99 counties and 100% beautiful—and never more so than in spring. The Brushy Creek Watershed in Carroll County is proof of that.

Uh-Oh...
Double Trouble

Meet the winners in our Pets & People Look-Alike Contest.

OUR STAFF did a double take when we saw this photo (right) of Cole Berka and boy's best friend "Shamus".

Then, after we stopped chuckling, we named them the winners of our "Pets & People Look-Alike Contest".

Our subscribers gave *thousands* of *Our Iowa* gift subscriptions at Christmastime. So for the benefit of these new readers, here's some background on the contest:

We've seen features in newspapers and on television that show people and their pets actually beginning to look alike.

No one knows if it's a coincidence…or whether, when people choose their pets, they tend to choose one with features that are "familiar".

Maybe friends begin thinking the two look alike because the pet develops similar habits and tendencies.

Whatever the case, we were curious whether this was true in parts of Iowa as well. So we announced a Pets & People Look-Alike Contest in our last issue and invited subscribers to submit photos of themselves, friends or relatives and their pets.

Cole and Shamus won "paws down".

"My 2-year-old son, Cole, and my parents' dog Shamus seem to have a love/hate relationship," explains Ben Berka of Huxley. "Cole likes to chase him around and pull his hair and ears. But Shamus is always right back next to him, ready to play.

"Here they are sharing a 'time-out' together!"

They may be a troublesome twosome, but this contest was all in fun, so we figured they deserved a prize anyway.

As the winner, Shamus will receive five shipments of holiday doggie treats throughout the year from Bloom and Bark, one of our frequent advertisers from Keosauqua.

And just so Shamus won't have to share, we're sending Cole a jumbo-size box of what else but…Animal Crackers. Congratulations!

The Runners-Up

We also want to recognize a couple of runners-up in our contest, including Harold Fairbairn of Atlantic and his three dogs "Sadie", "Spike" and "Sherlock".

Funny how Harold's beard resembles Sherlock's facial hair. Or is it the other way around—Sherlock's whiskers match

THE EYES HAVE IT—and so do the whiskers as you study this photo of Harold Fairbairn of Atlantic and "Sherlock", the dog on the right. Harold's son Scott of Prairie City submitted this fun runner-up entry.

Harold's beard?

Either way, thanks to Harold's son Scott Fairbairn of Prairie City for snapping the photo.

Then there's the duo of Curt Mackie of Norwalk and his dog "Patches" looking out the window at the season's first snowfall.

The cocker spaniel may not look exactly like Curt, but the way he's standing there on his hind legs, there's no doubt Patches is a chip off the ol' block.

"Keep your paw prints off the window glass, guys!" we can almost hear Curt's wife, Twila, saying. Thanks, Twila, for snapping the photo. 🏠

TEACH OLD DOGS NEW TRICKS? We're not sure who taught who, but Norwalk resident Curt Mackie and "Patches" look comically alike in this runner-up photo.

GENTLE GIANT. Many Iowans remember Dick Sparrow of Zearing and his legendary 40-horse hitch. Meet his great-grandson Rylen Sparrow and his friend "Ollie", a Percheron who stands 18.2 hands tall at the shoulders (a hand equals 4 inches). We're guessing Rylen might stand about 7 hands—give or take a couple fingers.

Summer at Last...
So Much to Do and See

June's worth waiting for. It's as though someone took crayons to spread different hues of green across our landscape. And it's barefoot time again!

Can you really *hear* corn grow? Many farmers contend they can when a sunny day follows a soaking rain. They say they often hear stalks *squeak* on days like that.

June's the official start of summer—it's the growing season, so there's plenty of work to get done. Most gardeners and farmers are eager to do it and to see the results.

The corn's likely to be over knee high by the Fourth of July ...the heirloom tomatoes are now showing promise...strawberries are ripe for picking...*and just look at those flowers!*

Early summer in Iowa is downright delightful. There's still springtime freshness in the air...gentle breezes rustle the cottonwoods down by the creek...and voices of children fill the air as they bike and play ball well into the evenings. Ah, summer!

If you're too busy for a drive to see all that's happening in the countryside, turn the pages ahead for our "armchair tour", with photos so vivid you'll feel you're *there*.

SOOTHING SCENES. Wagonload of flowers adds colorful touch to backyard hammock. Far left, rising sun in Washington County signals birth to a new day and start of a new crop season.

CLOTHED IN FINERY are the hillsides in summertime, when Queen Anne's lace and wild chicory color the landscape, like here in Adams County.

IDYLLIC IOWA. As cottony clouds float overhead, a farmstead nestled in the rolling hills of Jackson County near Baldwin basks in the Iowa sun.

Joseph Stanski

Gerald Rowles

NATURE HAS A SENSE OF HUMOR as evidenced by this cygnet in the catbird seat on mama swan.

BEFITTING ROYALTY. A royal throne might cost a king's ransom, but pales in comparison to these zinnias on which monarch butterflies are feeding in a flower garden at Bentonsport.

IOWA'S SUPERHIGHWAY isn't I-80, but rather the Mighty Mississippi. Just one 15-barge tow hauls the equivalent of 870 semitruck loads of grain!

Gerald Rowles

PUTTING THE HORSE BEFORE THE CART and clip-clopping along at 10 mph. That's the way to see the countryside near Frytown in Johnson County.

Gerald Rowles; photo above: Joseph Stanski

FARMALL

70th Annual
QUIMBY
'WATERMELON DAYS
JUNE 27, 28 2014
TRACTOR SHOW 10:00 am Saturday
TRACTOR PARADE
3:00 pm Saturday

Beth Wolterman

SLICE OF IOWA LIFE. You can't beat small-town celebrations and festivals for good food and down-home summer fun. So why not check out the hoedowns in your neck of the woods?

NO TRAFFIC JAMS HERE! Wildflowers color the roadside ditches and cottonwoods provide occasional canopy on a quiet country road near the Adams-Adair county line. Now, this is Iowa!

ON CLOUD NINE. Who wouldn't be on cloud nine...or ten...or twelve...surrounded by black-eyed Susans as far as the eye can see on a sunny afternoon in Wapello County?

PURGATORY CREEK in Carroll County looks like a fun stream to explore. Many young Iowans have no doubt conjured up Huck Finn-type adventures as they roamed its banks.

WALLFLOWERS. Nothing says summer like a trellis covered with clematis blossoms at Grandma's house.

116

Joseph Stanski

IN FULL SWING of a summer's eve, children make the most of the remaining daylight near Maquoketa in Jackson County. It's a scene that's played out across Iowa this time of year.

IT LOOKS LIKE A BIN BUSTER of a crop is on the way in Washington County, where vast acres of corn soak up the life-giving energy of the sun and thrive in the rich prairie soil.

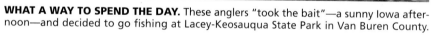

WHAT A WAY TO SPEND THE DAY. These anglers "took the bait"—a sunny Iowa afternoon—and decided to go fishing at Lacey-Keosauqua State Park in Van Buren County.

GOOD FENCES MAKE GOOD NEIGHBORS. So goes an old adage...and if it's true, the Jackson County farmer who built this beauty of a fence ought to be a neighborhood favorite. It's located along scenic Highway 64 as you drive into Maquoketa from the west.

GOT THE BLUES? The sight of an indigo bunting is sure to bring cheer. He looks as pretty as a parakeet.

OUR IOWA

Ty Smedes; next page: Gerald Rowles

GREENER PASTURES. We can't imagine the grass getting any greener than on this Clayton County farm. These horses ought to thank their lucky horseshoes for being pastured there.

WILD WITH WILDFLOWERS. Doolittle Prairie State Preserve in Story County includes 220 native plants. It's also home to 31 butterfly species, thanks to the many wildflowers.

TURN THE PAGE for a glimpse of Grant Wood country near St. Donatus. Iowa's most renowned artist used the rolling farm fields and wooded hilltops found in Jones and Jackson counties as inspiration for some of his most famous paintings.

Gerald Rowles

DELICATE AS A DOILY is this Queen Anne's lace blooming along a country road in Cedar County.

ON YOUR MARK…GET SET…JUMP! Competitors cheer on their entry in the Fourth of July frog-jumping contest in Battle Creek. Looks like this fella has a leg up on the competition.

CALM BEFORE THE STORM—storm of activity, that is—on East Lake, part of the Iowa Great Lakes Region where throngs of Iowans flock for summer fun.

POTS O' GOLD at both ends of this rainbow? Our photographer counted himself lucky to witness this spectacle early one morning in Dallas County.

Joseph Stanski

Gerald Rowles; photo above: Larry Lindell

PLUM CRAZY for plump, juice-running-down-your-chin, fresh-off-the-tree plums. These beauties were ripening in a backyard in Jefferson County. Another of the joys of summertime in Iowa!

WATERFALLS IN IOWA? Surprisingly we are blessed with a number of them. One of the most spectacular is the 200-foot Dunnings Spring Falls at Decorah in scenic northeast Iowa.

OUR IOWA

Favorite photos from our readers...
and the stories behind them.

On the Count of Three...

"IT WAS a warm summer day, and my daughter and her friends made the most of it at our farm pond," writes Ida County Hawk-Eye Beth Wolterman. "They made quite a splash!"

Iowa's "Great Lakes" Are Great

"THIS SUNSET was a perfect ending to a perfect day," writes Jill Hamrick of Webb. "We bring our family to Iowa's Great Lakes region in Dickinson County every summer...staying at a cousin's cabin on Spirit Lake, where we spend our days hiking, biking, boating and playing in the water. What memories!"

Yikes! Not a Wise Move

"WE FOUND this owlet in my flower bed, and my husband, Allan, grabbed it before our dog got to it," explains Nancy Jacobsen of Corydon. "As luck would have it, I happened to be there with my camera just as the owl latched onto Allan's fingers with its sharp talons."

PORKER'S A CORKER. "Our daughter Elizabeth and her hog 'Bob' were having a 'thank you moment' at the end of the swine show at the county fair," notes Dainna Smith of Decorah. "She spent a lot of time washing and preparing Bob for the show."

POOPED PAPER SCRAPER. "We were remodeling our 100-year-old farmhouse, which meant scraping lots and lots of wallpaper," explains Kim Kuehner of Fredericksburg. "Judging by this snapshot, our 2-year-old son, Emmett, had had enough for one day!"

HORSE OF A DIFFERENT COLOR. "That's our grandson Chase McDonough at our St. Patrick's Day parade," says Ruth Hand of Emmetsburg. "I'm not sure which is more Irish—the green horse or Chase with his red hair. One thing's for sure—Chase keeps our Irish eyes smiling."

GOT MILK? "With milk carton in hand, my son Rhyis seems to be asking this cow for a refill," writes Kristy Polenske of Rapids City, Illinois. "The photo was taken back in Iowa, in Clinton County where I grew up, at Blanchard Dairy Farm."

The Prettiest Farm in Iowa

Nothing symbolizes our state like proudly primped and painted farmsteads. We showcase one of the prettiest in each issue of Our Iowa magazine.

THERE'S MORE than covered bridges brightening Madison County these days.

Over the past 10 years, Steve and Rhonda Bunnell of Earlham have colorfully painted their corner of the county, too, with a dazzling array of flowers and landscaping on this issue's "Prettiest Farm in Iowa".

•Earlham

Steve and Rhonda grew up as childhood friends and married in 1980. They began creating their modern farmstead in 2007 on bare land they bought from Steve's parents. His grandfather first purchased the farm in 1963.

"We were living on a farm 5 miles north of here, but after selling that land we decided to try living in town," says Steve.

"After only 6 months, we knew town life wasn't for us. We had already ordered a shed to store our machinery here, then decided to build a home out here, too. The location was perfect—I've always wanted to live on a paved road."

A Green Thumb's Dream

Rhonda was thrilled as well. She's loved to garden her entire life, and the spacious yard was ideal to gussy up with lots of

LOOKIN' OUT ON A FINE SUMMER DAY. Steve and Rhonda Bunnell (above) enjoy the Madison County countryside in every direction from their handsome gazebo, also shown in its full glory at left.

flower beds, shrubbery, trees and vegetable plots.

"I retired from a nursing career after we moved here, and eventually took the Master Gardener course through Madison County Extension," she notes.

"These days, I enjoy tending to my flowers and vegeta- ⌐⟶

THAT'S QUITE A WELCOME! By midsummer, "Pardon Me" daylilies and purple coneflowers offer a friendly greeting to anyone arriving on the yard.

Photos: Gerald Rowles

A GRAND VIEW FROM THE ROAD. Folks passing by the farm enjoy watching landscaping colors change with the seasons. The tractors are old-time favorites that Steve brings out for special occasions. Below: Rhonda's whimsical display by the front door welcomes you to the home.

LET'S PLAY! Two young grandsons have ruled this playhouse, but they now need to make room for a girly year-old granddaughter.

YOU CAN LOOK, BUT DON'T ENTER. The sign warns Steve and his farm buddies to steer clear of Rhonda's garden shed, but that doesn't keep the menfolk from admiring her lush pretty flowers outside.

bles, helping Steve with farm work and spending time with our daughters Sarah and Sue and our three grandchildren. A friend and I also sew quilts for the Quilts of Valor Foundation."

The couple hired a local business to help with their initial landscaping, but since then they've enjoyed adding more landscaping themselves.

Rhonda starts nearly all her own perennials over winter in plastic milk jugs that she sets outside in the snow.

"I plant several seeds in each of about 30 jugs, and they germinate by early spring," she explains. "Starting perennials this way saves room in my greenhouse and allows the plants to slowly acclimate to spring weather before they're transplanted."

Grows Boxes of Veggies

Rhonda has also found growing vegetables vertically on cattle panels and in box gardens to be a wonderful way to enjoy fresh summer produce.

The Bunnells appreciate the beauty and benefits of trees, and the first year they planted fast-growing Austree willows around the perimeter of the farmstead; they've since added dozens of evergreens throughout the yard.

A pergola made from old power poles, a greenhouse that Steve built Rhonda for Christmas, a cozy fire pit and an Amish-built gazebo all beautifully accent the well-manicured yard.

"The gazebo's been moved three times, and I'm not moving it again," jokes Steve.

Another attractive structure is Rhonda's heated garden shed. In here, she keeps outdoor plants alive over the winter, or gives new plants a head start before spring. The shed raised a few curious eyebrows when it was being built.

"Folks would stop and ask what we were building, and I would tell them it was a chicken house," laughs Steve. "So, Rhonda decided it needed a sign that says, 'Hen House—No Roosters Allowed'."

Steve and Rhonda grow corn, soybeans and about 50 acres ⤳

BOXED VEGGIES. Cabbage, Swiss chard, beets and flowering kale thrive in a box garden amid colorful perennials. Below: After being moved three times, the Amish-built gazebo has found a permanent home just a few steps from the beautifully paved patio west of the house.

CAN'T BEAT COUNTRY LIVING. Steve and Rhonda built their warm and open farm home near Earlham after deciding town life just wasn't for them.

of hay on the land they farm. Steve has been no-tilling crops since 1985 and maintains excellent waterways to help control soil erosion and slow water runoff.

"I hated seeing our soil end up in ditches from doing too much tillage," he states. "Plus, about a third of our land is in the Raccoon River watershed, and I like doing our part in protecting the water downstream."

The couple was about to begin another harvest and was feeling the excitement that comes with it.

"I've been combining corn and beans since I was 16 years old, and I still look forward to bringing in the year's bounty," Steve relates.

Rhonda serves as grain cart operator during harvest, but when done she is happy to get back to primping her yard on one of The Prettiest Farms in Iowa—for her own enjoyment and for the pleasure of others.

"If my flowers help someone passing by forget about the chaos in their life for even a moment, I feel I've served my purpose," she says.

AND THE SEARCH GOES ON...for the "Prettiest Farm in Iowa". If you have an attractive farmstead (or know of one in your area), send us a few snapshots and a letter describing it. If we choose to feature it, we'll send out a professional photographer to take pictures for a future issue.

Mail to: "Prettiest Farm", *Our Iowa*, 1510 Buckeye Ave., Ames IA 50010. Or e-mail: *editors@OurIowaMagazine. com* and put "Prettiest Farm" in the subject line.

NO BATHING TODAY...but the birds likely won't mind, since they can admire these pretty Gaillardia Arizona Sun petals in their bath.

'It Was One Heckuva Ride!'

An Iowan landed a dream job traveling with the famous Anheuser-Busch Clydesdales.

By Lynn Betts

LIFE changed in a hurry for Loren Knoche just days before Christmas 14 years ago. That's when he signed on with Anheuser-Busch as a handler with the brewer's famous eight-horse Clydesdale hitch.

Dundee

"It was December 23 when I got a phone call out of the blue from their headquarters in St. Louis," Loren recalls. "They told me they were shorthanded and wanted me to start work the next day. To this day, I have no idea how they got my name.

"But I was divorced, my children were grown and living away from home and just by chance, I had already rented out my farm near Wheatland for the next year. So I told the company that it was something I'd like to do if they would give me a few days to get ready."

Loren sold his cow herd to a neighbor the following day, and his dad agreed to care for Loren's own horses that he kept at the farm. Three days after Christmas, he was on a plane headed for Phoenix to join one of the crews.

Had Never Strayed Far from Home

"I could probably count on my fingers the number of nights I'd been away from the farm in my 30 years of farming," says Loren. "I didn't even own a suitcase. I bought one, packed it and didn't unpack it again for 11-1/2 years until I retired in 2010.

"Anheuser-Busch likes to hire Iowa people—we had a half dozen Iowans working as handlers while I was there. My first

HORSE HAPPY. Loren Knoche enjoys horses, whether it was driving the Clydesdale hitch at Busch Stadium (above), or now on his Dundee acreage (right).

event showing the Clydesdales was at a fiddle festival in Casa Grande, Arizona."

In his first years with the hitch, Loren was on the road working 6 days a week, 11 months out of the year.

"It was a year before I got back to Iowa," Loren says. "I really didn't know what I was getting into, other than I'd be working with the Clydesdales."

Loren and his team were constantly on the go, sometimes getting the horses ready before daylight and working until 11 at night. It wasn't unusual to work a 15-hour day.

"But I loved it. We were either with the horses or out in the public nearly every day," Loren explains. "We would hitch up the horses about anywhere they could block off a street for us, and it was our job to show those beautiful Clydesdales to people wherever we went."

Loren knew all about harnessing and working with horses from his days of handling his own on the farm. But getting a feel for working with the public took some getting used to.

"I found out it's not as easy to harness the public as it is

132

horses," Loren laughs. "We were always concerned for people's safety. The Clydesdales were docile, but they could get scared and step on someone if people gathered around them too closely.

"We answered questions all day long. Sometimes you'd scratch your head at some of the things people would ask, but we were representing Anheuser-Busch so we went out of our way to please the public."

These Horses Are Huge!

Loren says the most frequent questions he got were about the size and weight of the horses.

To be part of the hitch, a Clydesdale has to weigh at least 2,000 pounds and measure 18 hands to its withers. One hand is 4 inches, so if you were to hop up on a Clydesdale to ride, as Loren often did, you'd be swinging your leg over the horse's back at a height 6 feet off the ground.

The Budweiser Clydesdales must also be bay colored, have four white legs, a white stripe in the face and a black mane and tail.

As the largest Clydesdale breeder in the world, Anheuser-Busch owns around 300 of the animals. The company always has plenty of stock from which to choose to get the exact markings they're looking for.

Loren worked on one of six hitches that Anheuser-Busch usually had out across the United States at any one time.

"Our crew took three semis down the road," says Loren. "The first carried four horses and the portable stalls. The second semi had six horses on board—that's the one I always drove. The third hauled the show wagon and all our tack. We also had a chase vehicle with all our personal gear."

Driving the Hitch Was Fun

Most trips began on a Monday, and the crew wouldn't drive more than 500 miles a day. They'd often overnight the horses at a local fairground.

"When we'd arrive at a destination, the first thing we did was get the horses out of the trucks," Loren says. "Tuesday was prep day, when we'd wash, clip and curry the horses. Then we'd show them four or five times the rest of the week. We brought 10 horses with us but only used eight on a hitch.

"I liked driving the hitch—that was the best part of the job. I didn't know I was going to get to do that, because I had never driven an eight-horse hitch before. But they let me start driving in places I couldn't get into trouble about 3 months into the job."

Loren was never the lead driver, but he sat tall in the second driver seat, dressed in his green uniform, and was often handed the reins.

"I loved feeling the power of those magnificent Clydesdales, each one weighing 2,000 pounds and with the strength to pull twice their weight. I liked the challenge of taking them through a tight spot, too, like a narrow street in a city."

Loren says every Clydesdale had a name, and not just because it was something cute for the public to hear.

"They had to have a name, a short one, because you can't touch the horses while you're driving them," Loren explains. "You have to call out their name to get them to do what you want.

"I remember Scott being a really good horse to work with, along with Bud, Jim and Levi."

Saw Lots of Country

Loren drove the hitch in several Mardi Gras parades, the Gator, Sugar and Cotton Bowl parades and in a Super Bowl parade in Tampa, Florida.

"We drove in a lot of St. Patrick's Day parades, too," says Loren. "Those were a lot of fun because the parade-watchers were always having a pretty good time."

Loren celebrated his 50th birthday in the desert in Mexico, where their Clydesdales were quarantined for 5 days before they could re-enter the United States after an exhibition south of the border.

More than once he rubbed shoulders with Tony La Russa, former manager of the St. Louis Cardinals baseball team, as the Budweiser wagon carried him to home plate at Busch Stadium on the opening day of the baseball season.

Loren's hitch even helped deliver the World Series trophy to home plate in Busch Stadium one year, which was a real treat for him since he played a lot of baseball for Wheatland High School as a teenager.

Small-Town Folks Were Friendly

"We were in every state east of Denver, in the biggest cities like New York and Chicago and in the smallest of towns like those right here in Iowa," Loren recalls. "People appreciated seeing us everywhere we went, but none more so than those in a small town.

"Those folks were thrilled that we'd come to their town or county fair, and they always had plenty of time to talk with us. It never cost these towns or fairs a cent to have us show up, either. The area Anheuser-Busch distributors paid our way."

Loren officially retired from the job in 2010, but if it hadn't been for a bad shoulder that needed surgery, he might still be caring for the Clydesdales today.

"Anheuser-Busch likes to hire Iowa people—we had a half dozen Iowans working as handlers..."

"Part of my job was to collar and bridle those huge geldings," says Loren. "The collar alone weighs 75 pounds, and all the harness together weighs 130 pounds. One day I felt my shoulder go out—I tore the rotator cuff. After that, I just couldn't lift the collars up over my head anymore.

"If that hadn't happened, I'd probably still be on the road with the Budweiser hitch. I'm happy to be back home in Iowa, but traveling with the Clydesdales was a great job."

"Doc" Rode High on the Wagon

Out on the road, folks often asked Loren if he would like to be a Clydesdale in another life, since they were such a majestic animal.

"I'd laugh and tell them no, I'd much rather be 'Doc', the Budweiser Dalmatian who rode with us on the wagon," Loren chuckles. "Doc went with us wherever we'd go and got treated well.

"Once at the Minnesota State Fair, Doc was following a small boy who had a hot dog in his hand. Doc watched the boy's every move, and pretty soon he had snatched the hot dog out of the boy's hand."

Loren continues: "The boy didn't mind, but his mother sure got excited. She yelled, 'Hey, that dog just took my boy's hot dog!'

"I told her, 'That's okay, ma'am, the hot dog won't hurt him.' Doc had a pretty good life."

Today, Loren lives outside Dundee on an acreage that has a horse barn where he keeps his Quarter Horse, "Charlie", who's about half the size of a Clydesdale, and a few other horses he trains.

"Even though I'm retired, I buy a few horses, break them to ride and then sell them," says Loren. "This horse stuff gets in your blood, and you can't get it out."

Iowa Rewind

A glimpse at our past from Iowans' family photo albums.

EACH ISSUE of *Our Iowa* includes this "Iowa Rewind" section, featuring old-time photos that chronicle Iowa's rich history and portray a way of life we still proudly treasure today.

We'd like to consider some of *your* cherished photos as well of family, friend or special events from yesteryear.

So browse through your old albums, and if you have an interesting snapshot from the 1920s through the 1970s that helps tell the story of Iowa's heritage, send it in so we can share it with readers in future issues.

Please include any information you have about the photo, such as names of the people or event pictured, location, year it

was taken and anything else that explains why the photograph is special to you.

To avoid your photo being lost or damaged in the mail, we suggest having a high-resolution scan made of it and e-mailing it to: *editors@OurIowaMagazine.com*. Put "Iowa Rewind" in the subject line.

Or, make a copy of the photo and send it to: "Iowa Rewind", *Our Iowa*, 1510 Buckeye Ave., Ames IA 50010.

If it's an original that you would like returned, please include a self-addressed stamped envelope, and we'll make sure your photo gets sent back to you.

GRANDMA'S PUTTIN' THE SQUEEZE ON. "It was unusual for my grandma Cora Wohlenberg to milk the family's two cows, but she was determined to show Grandpa Pete that she knew how it was done at their home in Everly in 1940," chuckles Orpha Matthiesen from Dysart. "I think the look on Grandpa's face is just priceless."

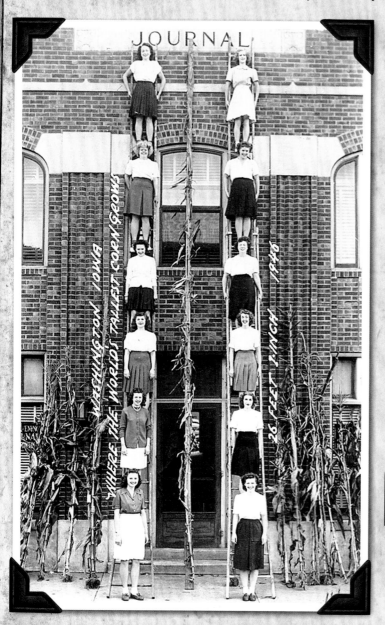

STANDING TALL. "These girls from Washington High School found a fun way to show off the tallest corn in the area in 1946—this stalk measured 26 feet, 1 inch," writes Jane Amos of Clarks Summit, Pennsylvania. "My mom, Fern Mendenhall of Columbus Junction, is second from the top on the right."

NEITHER RAIN, NOR MUD, NOR RUTTED ROADS would stop Elgin mail carrier Phil Moser and his horse from delivering the mail in rural northeast Iowa in the early 1900s. "My grandfather Alfred Jacob Sr. was a fellow carrier at the time, and he and Phil were eager to begin using cars on their routes," writes Marilyn Schaer of Elgin.

ONE PLANK AT A TIME. Harry Smith and R.C. Story work high above an 80-foot-deep ravine as they rebuild the 262-foot swinging bridge in Columbus Junction in 1922 in this photo sent by Jim Gabriel of Kearney, Missouri. The original bridge was built in 1886.

THE HEADLESS HORSE. "I'm not sure if this horse was camera shy or just being ornery when he turned his head as this photo was taken in 1920," chuckles Connie Schroder of Avoca. "That's my grandpa Ernest Peters standing atop the horse on our family farm near Shelby."

TURN THE PAGE and see a beautiful farmstead in Dubuque County complete with a 2-acre pond stocked with fish. Photo by Gerald Rowles.

"HOW MUCH IS THAT DOGGIE IN THE WINDOW..." Little Sophie Madden is too young to remember that famous Patti Page hit from the '50s. "Our granddaughter and our pug 'Daisy' were looking out the door, just yearning to play with our Weimaraner 'Emma' out on the farm," explain Gary and Brenda Madden of Ringsted.

THE WHOLE HERD HEARD HER. "I was home from the big city visiting my parents, and as we were having coffee one morning, I spotted 'Fiona', one of my parents' donkeys," relates Krista Link of Eden Prairie, Minnesota. "When I called to her, all of the goats looked up in a curious and comical way as I snapped a photo."

CATAPULT RIGHT OUT THE WINDOW. "Our cat 'Stella' must have had a serious case of cabin fever the day I snapped this photo," notes Julie King of Des Moines. "She couldn't wait to get a whiff of spring air. Then again, maybe she was eyeing a bird in the yard. It's hard to tell exactly what cats are thinking."

LIP SERVICE? "That's our son Colton going nose to nose with a llama named 'Curious George', " says Kim Baker of Carroll. "We call him Curious George because he is so inquisitive with everyone and everything. The photo was taken at a gathering of my wife's family who live near Halbur. We cherish our family gatherings and get together as often as we can."

Cardinal Guards Old Glory

"I SPOTTED this mama cardinal in my parents' flower gardens," explains Alicia Smith of Colo. "The cardinals made their nest in Bob and Marilyn Longs' abandoned greenhouse in Colo. We had a great view from their porch."

How Sweet It Is!

MESSY? WHO CARES? "It's the start of the sweet corn season in Iowa, and my son Carson enjoys the early spoils of summer on our family's deck in Adel," notes Michelle Waddingham. "Juicy, buttery sweet corn—a succulent treat after a swim."

Walking Tall

"THIS IS our grandson Eli John on our farm in rural Dumont last fall," says Shelly Codner. "The caption I have given the photo is: Locally grown and certified adorable (by Grandpa and Grandma)."

Nothing to Crow About

"I HAD JUST finished staining this old garden bench that my husband made for me and, of course, these guys all decided it was time to lounge on it," writes Ann Meyer of Cedar Falls. "Come on, give me a break!"

GOT AN EYE-POPPIN' PICTURE? If you have an appealing photo of Iowa's beautiful scenery or that depicts Iowa life, send it to: "Iowa Eye-Catchers", *Our Iowa*, 1510 Buckeye Ave., Ames IA 50010.

Or e-mail it to: *editors@OurIowaMagazine.com* and put "Eye-Catchers" in the subject line.

Small-Town Cartoonist Draws on Laughs

Iowa's only national magazine cartoonist sketches gags in a tiny back-porch office in Emmetsburg.

SOME PEOPLE like to doodle on napkins or place mats, drawing lighthearted sketches of this or that. Others enjoy telling short jokes. Not many of them would consider combining the two talents...and try to make a living at it.

Dave Carpenter does.

Leaning over a drawing board in an office so small he likely can stretch his arms and touch both walls, Dave starts each day—and ends it—turning out sketches he hopes will make people laugh. It's his "job".

He's a full-time magazine cartoonist, the only one in Iowa. After working at his trade for 36 years, he's very good at it. In fact, he makes a decent living cranking out cartoons for a slew of national magazines.

Among his regular buyers have been publications such as *The Wall Street Journal*, *Good Housekeeping*, *Forbes*, *The Saturday Evening Post*, *Better Homes & Gardens*, *Barron's*, *Harvard Business Review*, *National Enquirer*, *Country Woman*, *Farm & Ranch Living*, *Ebony*, *American Legion* and more.

But it's likely most national magazine editors in their high-towered offices haven't a clue the gags they're buying originate from an isolated artist, crafting 20 to 30 new cartoons a week in his tiny "studio" on the back porch of his home in Emmetsburg.

Our subscribers get their grins regularly from Dave's cartoons in each issue of *Our Iowa*. We also call on him often for humorous sketches that illustrate articles.

How He Got Started

Dave enjoyed drawing as a child, as do most children. He'd trace pictures from coloring books and redraw characters from the *Des Moines Register* comics. It wasn't until college he began taking art seriously.

"I was attending the University of South Dakota," he relates. "But I kept finding myself doodling cartoons in my dorm when I should have been studying. I finally decided to see if I could turn cartooning into a career."

From Grocer to Grinner

So he put off college and worked in a grocery store by day while practicing his art by night. Finally, he sent five cartoons to several magazines...and waited.

"A couple weeks later, I received a check in the mail. It was only for $10, but

---

> *"What can be more gratifying than making thousands of people laugh?"*

I'd sold my first cartoon! I was *estatic*. And when I received the magazine with my printed cartoon, I was *hooked!*"

Today, 36 years later, Dave creates and submits around 350 new cartoons each year. While most magazines pay $100 to $300, a few pay up to $800.

Dave really can't explain how he comes up with ideas for cartoons. He usually carries a notebook to jot down pieces of conversation or a cute phrase that might have potential...and sometimes uses restaurant napkins.

He contends coming up with the "gag line" is the most important part of the cartoon. "It's about 99% gag and 10% drawing. The editor is buying the joke, and the drawing simply helps the joke."

Studies What Tickles Editors

His next step is to study a publication to review its previous cartoons, to get an idea of the type of humor they're seeking.

"That gets my mind thinking in a humorous way. I'll select my 10 best gags and start making rough pencil sketches 'til I feel they deliver the gag line, then trace them over the pencil lines with a pen.

"I'll put all 10 of these cartoons in the mail, then while waiting on the outcome of that group, I'll start on another set for another magazine. Then another...then another. That's how I make a living.

"I enjoy the independence of being my own boss and working at my own pace. I also enjoy the challenge and creative element. And when it leads to a published cartoon, it's very gratifying.

"What can be better than providing a lighthearted moment and making thousands of people across the country laugh at something your created?"

(Dave proved he doesn't take himself seriously by providing the selfie below.)

DAVE DRAWING DAVE.

Memories of Illegal Liquor Still Linger

The legend lives on as stories of Prohibition whiskey improve with age.

FOR such a small town, Templeton (pop. 332) has a big history. Times were tough for farmers after World War I.

Templeton

To support their families and make their farm payments, more than a few turned to brew.

That is, a number of Templeton area farmers began distilling their own rye whiskey, and apparently did it well. Aptly named Templeton Rye, it gained the nickname "the Good Stuff" for its high quality and smooth finish.

This was the Prohibition Era, and plenty of this illegal liquor was shipped to Chicago by train along with loads of cattle, on cattle trucks and other inventive ways. The Templeton undertaker even filled his hearse with it for deliveries!

The homemade hooch even caught the attention of gangster Al Capone, who began distributing it to local establishments in the Windy City, where it had a sterling reputation for quality.

Said one Windy City tavern owner at the time, "If you asked for a bottle of the finest whiskey in Chicago, that's what the bartender would offer you—Templeton Rye."

And if visitors to the city happened to mention they were from Iowa, they were sure to be asked how close they lived to Templeton. Even today, the locals recall the stories shared by those who well remember those days when the Feds were feared.

Steam Raised Suspicion

Scott Bush, who reintroduced Templeton Rye in 2005, shares one of the tall tales: "My great-grandfather had a still on his farm, and my grandpa remembers a visitor expressing concerns—the visitor noted that smoke was coming from the roof of one of the barns, and it was the only one without snow on the roof.

"My great-grandfather quickly explained that building was the hog barn, and the large number of hogs produced a lot of heat. But, of course, the heat was coming from the still."

Merlyn Zubrod of Templeton has even more personal memories: "My dad didn't make the liquor, but he was one of those who stored it. I remember he told us kids not to go into the hog barn. I didn't know why—we no longer were raising any hogs. I learned later the barn was filled with whiskey."

Merlyn became aware later how scared his mom was during those times, and also learned his dad was paid $100 for the storage. "Like a lot of other folks, we were really poor at the time, and that was a lot of money then," he explains. "Dad said he slept with that $100 under his pillow the night he got it."

Buried in Caves

The hog barn wasn't the only place the liquor was hidden, Merlyn says. "I was walking in our grove and found one of our cows had fallen through some wooden flooring covered with grass. Below it was a cave full of whiskey barrels! I ran to get Dad, and he hitched up a horse and pulled her out with a chain."

The topper of all stories, though, relates to a large tombstone in the Templeton cemetery, which has been somewhat of a tourist attraction now that the town's namesake whiskey is being poured again. It's the gravesite of a local priest, Father Bernard Schulte.

The sizable marker has a small "door" on its side—and the three bolts on it are noticeably well worn...for good reason. During the Prohibition days, bottles of Templeton Rye were stored in that hollowed-out tombstone.

Says Merlyn, "Guess the locals figured the Feds wouldn't look there."

SHHH! Only a few of the locals were privy to Templeton Rye in the early days.

GRAVE CONCERN. During Prohibition, whiskey was hidden inside local priest's tombstone. Photos show front and side view; inset reveals the worn bolts on its removable side door.

The Old Farmer Sez...

"Children rarely misquote. They usually repeat word for word what you shouldn't have said."

Highway Signs Yield Miles of Smiles

Drivers chuckle while reading our roadside signs posted in every county in Iowa.

OUR longtime readers often tell us how much they enjoy our Burma-Shave-like signs.

They still grin broadly when they see lighthearted verses such as: **Around the corner...lickety-split... beautiful car...wasn't it?**

With our continued growth in subscribers, we've learned some newer readers are curious how these signs came about. So here's a bit of background:

As our regulars know, one of our goals from the outset with *Our Iowa* magazine has been to add a little fun to the lives of our audience...and to ours as well. So we keep coming up with wild ideas and say, "Why not?" The Burma-Shave signs are one of those ideas.

Both of us silver-haired editors vividly remember those rhyming signs that brought humor to highways across the country during the '50s, with jingles so clever some seniors still remember them today.

Such as: **Ben met Anna...made a hit...neglected beard... Ben-Anna split.** And then the familiar Burma-Shave logo would appear on the last sign.

So, we thought it would be fun to bring back that "slice of Americana" by posting a single set of these nostalgic signs in each of Iowa's 99 counties, each with a different original Burma-Shave rhyme.

That would make each set of signs an *exclusive*—and make Iowa the *only* state in the nation with roadside signs adding smiles to miles for drivers. That was 6 years ago. Seemed like a good idea, so we went ahead.

"Please, Choose Our Town!"

Instead of selecting sites at random, we asked small-town leaders to write and indicate their interest. We felt having the only set in their county might bring some business traffic their way. (It has—readers have told us they count how many sets they can find, then stay for lunch and shopping.)

In some counties, we soon had multiple towns *vying* for the signs. In those cases, we selected the site based on its location and how convinced we were that the townspeople would maintain the signs after they were up.

And that's worked well, too. Our readers quickly report when a sign is damaged, missing or not standing straight.

We continually hear how much people love these rhyming jingles. Such as: **Slow down, George...sakes alive...Helen missed... signs four and five.**

The only difference between the originals is that ours have *Our Iowa* posted on the last sign. After all, Burma-Shave no lon-

ger exists, so it doesn't need the attention...and we do.

"People in my area always tell me they enjoy looking for the signs when they're out on a drive," says Sharon Larson, our Allamakee County field editor. "And the locals proudly look after them. When two signposts were damaged by snowplows, the group in charge of the signs had them fixed in 24 hours."

"I love these signs! They remind me of riding in the back of my parents' car and we all read the verses together out loud— and very loud!" writes Karen Lenniks of Red Oak.

"These signs bring back fond memories for older people, and I think it offers a chance for a bit of bonding when they explain the 'Burma-Shave days' to family members and younger friends. I think it's cool that Iowa's the only state with these signs."

NOT POSTA DO THAT...but this couple did while putting up signs in Union County. Local groups in all 99 counties found this a fun project.

Iowa Was Calling

Even the mountains couldn't keep this reader away when all the signs said that it was time to come home.

THE RAINBOW'S END shows a pretty photo by Don Wellington of Sac City. For the author, the pot of gold is Iowa.

By Ruth Steinkoenig, Laurens

THOUGHTS flood my mind of growing up in Iowa and I feel so blessed to have been born back in 1934, when life was simple.

Lake City is where I made my debut into the world. In our house, it was a time of no furnace, no running water, no bathroom and definitely no television.

We did have a radio that we all gathered around to hear wonderful music programs and serials. I loved getting ready for school in the mornings while listening to *Cowboy Ken* and washing dishes to the accompaniment of great singers on *The Railroad Hour*.

We didn't need cell phones for our social media. We got all the news from walking to school with our friends or meeting them afterward at the local soda fountain, where we enjoyed a Coke for a nickel. If we had a dime, we'd have a "mud", which featured ice cream and chocolate syrup in our Coke.

Of course, we didn't do this every day—most of us only got 10 cents a week for our allowance. Many times we spent our coin on Saturday nights as we all gathered around the gazebo in the park, where we listened to band music and mingled with friends.

Learned Many Lessons

We received an excellent education, both from school and farm life. I sometimes wondered if Dad didn't realize that he had four girls, because he taught us to work just like he would've with four boys. I'm glad, though, because the hard work was good for us.

Our school gave us opportunities to excel in sports and music, as well as sewing and secretarial courses. I made most of my clothes using the beautiful materials that came with the bags of chicken feed.

Wouldn't kids of today laugh themselves silly at the thought of wearing such things? Don't laugh, kids. We were the best-dressed in school, because our dad raised hundreds of chickens, and we wore the fringe benefits.

Promised to Return

I was blessed with many adventures in Iowa, from education to marriage and children. But after the death of my young husband, I thought a change of scenery would be good for my family. I found my way to another adventure in the beautiful state of Colorado.

As we left, I silently promised, "Iowa, I will be back."

Fast-forward 30 years, and life was good, but sometimes our plans are interrupted by unexpected changes. A serious bout with pneumonia and damage to the old lungs brought about instructions from the doctors to move to a lower altitude.

While I loved the majestic mountains, my new friends and our lovely home, my lungs did not. So my new husband and I began the search for a new home.

There was no question in my mind where we should go. It was as if the state remembered my promise—Iowa was calling.

Happy to Be Back

Upon my return, I was overwhelmed with a feeling of thankfulness for arriving back where I first began.

I thought back to the lessons I learned in Iowa as a child that had given me the strength to face so many adversities. Strict parents plus strict but caring teachers in church and school instilled within me the guidelines and faith for a successful life. That small-town love and support was a great foundation.

Iowa had not changed in my absence. Those friendly people were still there, waiting to welcome me back with open arms.

I am glad that I left for a time, because leaving Iowa taught me how much I loved it.

The same could be said about many aspects of life. Because I grew up without modern conveniences, not a day goes by when I don't appreciate the wonderful conveniences we all have in our homes today.

Although I do miss standing around the dishpan and wiping dishes dry while listening to a favorite program on the radio. Maybe I will start washing dishes in the sink so I can recall the joys of years gone by…or maybe not.

Either way, I'm glad to be back where all those memories began. Iowa, I owe you a big one!

WHO'S NEXT? If you've returned to Iowa after living elsewhere—or know of someone who has—share the story with our readers. Send a letter to: "Why I Came Back to Iowa", *Our Iowa*, 1510 Buckeye Ave., Ames IA 50010.

Or send an e-mail to: *editors@OurIowaMagazine.com* and put "Why I Came Back to Iowa" in the subject line.

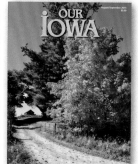

Our Iowa magazine was launched 10 years ago, in the fall of 2007. Here and on the following page is a colorful lineup of all 60 front covers we've featured since then.

Two things make this magazine unique: It's supported primarily by subscriptions, not advertising. And it's pretty much "written by readers", allowing Iowans to "chat with each other" on a regular basis. This book provides many good samples of that.

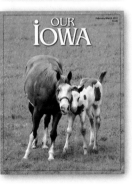

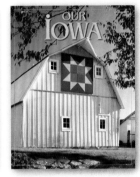
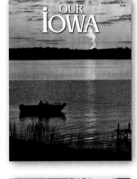

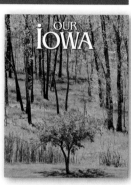

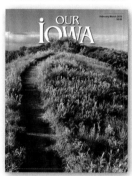
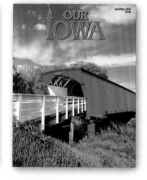